S0-BED-418

Software
Easter Eggs

David Nagy-Farkas

Abacus

www.abacuspub.com

Copyright © 1997

Abacus
5370 52nd Street SE
Grand Rapids, MI 49512

www.abacus.pub.com

Printed in the U.S.A.

ISBN 1-55755-326-2

10 9 8 7 6 5 4 3 2 1

Table Of Contents

Table Of Contents

Table Of Contents

Table Of Contents

Table Of Contents

Part II Existing Easter Eggs
127-238

Table Of Contents

x

Table Of Contents

XI

Table Of Contents

Table Of Contents

XIII

Table Of Contents

Part I

Introduction To Easter Eggs

Introduction

Chapter 1

Introduction

Two years ago if you had asked me what an Easter egg was, I would have replied with the typical answer—those dyed eggs that children (and some others) get excited about on Easter Sunday. Or how about the chocolate eggs the Cadbury bunny lays? It certainly wouldn't have anything to do with computers. However, a year and a half ago my whole concept of an "Easter egg" changed dramatically. A good friend of mine, John Pottebaum, called me up as I was doing some programming. He sounded really excited:

"You won't believe what I found in Excel 95!"

Being in a "coding" mindset and trying to find a frustratingly elusive error in my code, my curiosity was only mildly piqued. At the time, John was working for Microsoft and I figured he just found some nifty new feature—interesting, but hardly something about which even John would get impassioned. He seemed too excited.

"What did you find?" I asked, somewhat blandly.

Introduction

"There's a (bleep)ing Doom engine inside Excel! You can walk around in this 3-D world and see the programmers' names scrolling on the walls. You can even look up and down!" he replied.

"Yeah, right," I said unbelievingly.

"No, it's true! I swear! I'll prove it to you!"

> I couldn't imagine people writing something similar just to hide it inside a completely unrelated program like Excel.

I had a hard time believing John because Doom is a big and complex program. By now, I'm sure all of you have at least heard of Doom, the classic 3-D action game that has spawned a million clones. Doom was a huge feat of programming at the time, and I couldn't imagine people writing something similar just to hide it inside a completely unrelated program like Excel. That this complex 3D engine had been incorporated into a major Microsoft product was simply inconceivable. But the mention of proof had gotten my attention.

"Prove it? How?"

"You've got Excel on your machine, don't you?" he inquired.

"Yeah I do, and I'm in front of my computer right now."

"Okay," he said, "just do exactly what I tell you:

1. Start up Excel 95.

2. Use the arrow keys on your keyboard--NOT your mouse--to go down to the 95th row of the spreadsheet.

3.   Highlight the entire row. You can use your mouse for this: just click on the row number on the left.

4.   Hit Tab to move to column B.

5.   Using your mouse, go to the Help menu and select "About Microsoft Excel."

6.   Hold down Ctrl and Shift on your keyboard and click on the Tech Support button."

I followed his directions to the letter. Lo and behold, he was right! A window titled "The Hall of Tortured Souls" appeared. It contained the three dimensional world he described over the phone. I could walk around in this world, and the names of the Excel programmers were scrolling along some of the walls. Okay, so I couldn't shoot hordes of beasties with a rocket launcher, but it was still darn impressive. My love of Easter eggs awakened.

Naturally, something this cool had to be shared with all my friends. The next day at work, I showed my friend and co-worker Colby O'Donnell this nifty trick. "Cool Easter egg!" he said. "Easter egg? What's that?" I replied. It turned out that Colby knew a couple other wacky features programmers had smuggled into software and these tricks were affectionately dubbed "Easter eggs."

Within a few days of questioning friends and reading magazines, I had found Easter eggs in Windows 95, Windows 3.11, Microsoft Word, and two different versions of Microsoft Excel.

After more had been discovered, however, the magazines started to lighten up. They realized that a large number of products contain an Easter egg or two.

Even with this new attitude, however, Easter eggs still usually get treated as spawn of the "programming underworld," where a lone, wily programmer manages to sneak his or her tricks past the watchful and protecting eyes of fellow programmers and management. As we will see, this often is not the case, and entire development teams may collaborate in the creation of Easter eggs. Some even have management's approval!

> Today, Easter eggs have almost attained "feature" status among software developers.

Today, Easter eggs have almost attained "feature" status among software developers. Products seem incomplete if they don't contain an egg or two. In this age of megacorporations and huge design teams for single programs, Easter eggs have become a way for programmers to put some personality back into the software.

Authors use them to say, "Hey! There are real people behind this thing you're using! We're proud of our work and we hope you enjoy using this as much as we enjoyed designing it."

I have tried to go beyond a simple listing of Easter eggs with this book. This is a history of the Easter egg world and how they have evolved in complexity and humor over the years. Here are tips on how to find Easter eggs yourself, with methods catagorized by difficulty so you can find them whether you're a computer virgin or regularly do binary math in your head.

You will also be taken into the depths of the programming community to see how Easter eggs are conceived. Included are some rare glimpses of eggs that were intercepted by management and never saw the light of day.

So sit back, and enjoy the lighter side of software for a while. You'll discover that programmers like a good laugh as much as the rest of us.

What Easter Eggs Are

Chapter

2

Chapter 2

What Easter Eggs Are

Many misconceptions surround the definition of a software Easter egg. Some people think an Easter egg is what you get when you have hacked a program so that it will produce funny results. Others think cheat codes for games are Easter eggs. The truth is, most people have no clue because they've only heard the term used with painted chicken eggs in April.

Let's clear up all of this confusion right now. To be a true software Easter egg, a feature must satisfy the following five criteria:

It Must be Undocumented. Many people think that they've found an Easter egg just because they figured out some new feature of their accounting program, and didn't bother to read the manuals in the first place. True Easter eggs are unknown features and don't appear in any software documentation.

It Must have been Written by the Original Programmers. If some hacker gets his fingers into the code of your spreadsheet to make it perform bad math on new years day, it doesn't qualify as an Easter egg. The actual program code can't be modified in any way. Otherwise, somebody could legitimately go out and write an "Easter Egg Virus" that spreads around adding Easter eggs into software.

It Must be Reproducible. Just because you decided to delete some configuration files and now your terminal program beeps like mad whenever you open it, this doesn't mean you've found an Easter egg. Anybody, anywhere, should be able to take the same software through the same set of instructions and end up with the same results.

It Must Not Do Damage. Easter eggs are meant for fun. If some undocumented feature formats your hard drive without your knowledge, it doesn't qualify as an egg. That sort of thing is most likely a genuine bug, and should be reported to the manufacturer.

IT MUST BE ENTERTAINING! This is by far the most important qualification. Maybe a word processor has an undocumented feature that will spit out a document in ones and zeros instead of regular text. This was probably added as a debugging feature and the programmers forgot to take it out. Why would you want to see your document in binary? It's silly, and more importantly, it's *boring*. Give programmers a little credit. If they want to entertain you, their attempt will be pretty obvious.

Just five short rules—it sounds simple, doesn't it? But you would be amazed at how many people forget them and "discover" fake Easter eggs. Let's look at some actual examples.

Example 2-1

When you run Windows 95, if you hold down the ⌊Alt⌋ key and press ⌊Tab⌋, you will bring up a list of all the programs currently running on your system. You can switch between them by keeping ⌊Alt⌋ held down and pressing ⌊Tab⌋ repeatedly. When you are on the application you want to use, let go of the ⌊Alt⌋ key.

If you haven't used Windows much, this might seem like a pretty useful Easter egg. The problem is that it is so useful that it is actually a feature of Windows. From at least Windows 3.1, every version of Windows has allowed the user to "Alt-Tab" between the running applications. It's not the most commonly known feature, but it is documented, and all of the obsessive-compulsive computer manual readers out there probably spotted it right away.

Example 2-2

*Take the program file of application X and open it with a hex editor. Go down to address 0xAF398D28 and change the **4D** to **32**. The next time you run the program, notice the funny colors in the Help menu.*

This violates the "Original Programmer" rule. This is not an Easter egg because the original programmers didn't put it in the program. With enough hacking at bits and pieces of code, you can make any program do anything. To coin a phrase, "Hacking does not an Easter egg make."

Example 2-3

Set your Windows screen saver to Starfield Simulation. When the screen saver comes on, your monitor will make a high-pitched whining sound.

Maybe *your* monitor will, but I bet this won't happen for most people. The problem here is that the result is probably not reproducible, and is more likely due to a hardware idiosyncrasy than the software itself. If you think you've discovered an Easter egg, first tell a couple of friends about it. If they get it to work on their machines, you've probably struck pay dirt. Otherwise, a little visit to the PC doctor might be in order for your own computer.

Example 2-4

*Go to the DOS prompt. Type "deltree *.*" and answer Yes to all the questions that follow.*

Not only is this a documented feature of DOS, but it's also destructive. Destructive behavior is not allowed. If you follow the directions, you will erase everything on your hard drive. Be very wary of so-called "Easter eggs" that ask you to delete something to make them work. It most likely isn't an egg at all, but either a bug in the software, or a miscreant trying to pull a fast one on you.

Example 2-5

In PencilPad, press F11 *while holding* Ctrl *and* Alt. *The file you are editing will be reloaded from disk.*

This is an undocumented feature that is perfectly reproducible, and was put there by the original programmers. It even seems like it could be useful to some people. However, it violates the golden rule—it's *boring*. Would you call up your best friend at two in the morning and say, "Guess what?!? I found a secret way to reload my document in PencilPad!!!" Even if your friend was the biggest computer buff in the world, you would still deserve to get smacked around a little for waking him or her with such a discovery. This sounds like a genuine feature that wasn't documented, but it certainly wasn't put in for entertainment purposes.

Game Cheat Codes

Today, most computer games have certain tricks and codes that allow the player to cheat. Are these Easter eggs? They were certainly put there by the programmers, and they are reproducible and undocumented. Games are, by definition, wholly intended for entertainment, so each of their components, including cheat codes, must contribute to this. They seem to satisfy all of the requirements of an egg, so why single them out?

Cheat codes for games are a special case because they violate the entertainment rule in spirit. For a game to be fun, the player needs to overcome some obstacles and get a sense of accomplishment from beating the game. Cheat codes, while entertaining for some, actually remove the challenge from games. When the challenge is removed, a game is no longer fun. Entertainment is lost in the process, and cheat codes might be considered "anti-eggs."

> Some of the best Easter eggs are in games...

This isn't to say that games can't have Easter eggs in them as well. Game programmers have a greater opportunity than most to hide funny scenes and actions in their code. Some of the best Easter eggs are in games, and some cheat codes definitely have Easter egg elements.

For example, in Ultima 7, there is a cheat code that allows you to get any single item in the game. This allows you to create funny and absurd situations, like carrying a piece of ocean with rippling waves in your backpack. While it is possible to use the code to cheat, it also lets you do a lot of amusing things that you couldn't normally do within the game. When in doubt about whether an item in a game constitutes an egg, ask yourself these two questions:

- ◆ "Is the game more fun when using this feature or not using it?"

- ◆ "Can I do things or go places that were obviously never intended as part of the normal gameplay?"

That should resolve most indecisiveness. However, if you're still having trouble, maybe some examples will help.

Example 2-6

In the game Doom, type "IDKFA." You will get all weapons and ammunition, as well as all key cards.

This is a pretty clear-cut example of a cheat code that does NOT qualify as an Easter egg. You could get all the weapons, ammunition, and key cards by just playing the game well. There is nothing particularly out of the ordinary about that situation. This cheat code just makes the game less challenging. (Booo! REAL gamers don't need cheat codes.)

Example 2-7

In Doom II, type "IDCLIP" to walk through walls.

Normally, you can't walk through walls, so at least this code lets you do something that isn't normally possible in the game. But think about it; walking through walls is just a shortcut to traveling to places you could get to anyway. Granted, it might be pretty tough, with thousands of monsters in your path that you must mercilessly gun down, but that's the point of the game, right? This "egg" unquestionably gets a thumbs down.

Here's an easy one. This is not a cheat code but an obvious Easter egg in the program.

Example 2-8

1. Boot up Rise of the Triad on Christmas Day.

2. Start a level and it should play Christmas music.

3. One of the heroes will also have a red cap on his head.

4. Similar things will happen on other major holidays, such as Halloween.

This is an easy call. Do the Christmas music and red cap give you any unfair advantage? No, of course not, unless you think a red cap gives you "style" points or something. It's just there for fun. See, games can have genuine Easter eggs too, not just cheat codes!

Example 2-9

This is for Ultima VI:

1. Talk to Iolo.

2. Say "spam" 3 times, then say "humbug."

3. A cheat menu pops up. You can use this menu to modify your statistics and create any item in the game out of thin air.

I ran into this one myself a few years ago. Just reading the description, I would probably say this wasn't an Easter egg. But having seen it personally, it's a much closer call. Yes, I could use the menu to raise my stats and get cool weapons and armor. But it also lets you create ANY item in the game and put it in your inventory. This means anything from a table, to a tract of land, to a square of ocean water complete with rippling waves! I remember creating a bunch of water and throwing it down on the ground to create my own little

artificial pond. I could also throw these things at enemies and they would do damage! This cheat code has some definite Easter-egg-like possibilities. But it's still a tough call, and I'll leave it up to personal preference. What do you think?

How Easter Eggs Get Into Products

How can these hidden and usually useless features get into software? Why do programmers spend all this time and effort just for a little bit of humor? Why would management allow it?

In fact, Easter eggs are often not known to managers until it is too late to take them out. In modern software development, there are usually three groups of people working on the product:

◆ Managers

◆ Programmers

◆ Testers

This division of labor can be very efficient. Managers take care of the overall direction of the software's development. They also deal with marketers and go to all of the various company meetings so programmers and testers don't have to. Good management frees up programmers and testers to do their jobs effectively. And a good manager keeps the programmers and testers focused (so they don't spend all of their time on frivolous Easter eggs!).

21

Programmers take care of the actual software design and code writing. Plain and simple, they know how to write programs and that's what they do. Management tells them what needs to be done, and they do the nitty gritty work of putting plans into practice.

A good programmer or software engineer can be hard to come by. They are very skilled workers, similar to great craftsmen in any trade. You can tell an architect, "Build me a three bedroom house," and any architect could probably do it. A really good architect, however, would design a house considering many details and factors, such as the use of space, placement of stairways, windows and doors, the appearance from outside and inside, and your particular needs and desires.

Similarly, any programmer can write code, but a good programmer really "designs" a program. Hence, they can have a lot of personal pride in their creations.

Testers focus on running the final product through every possible scenario a user could produce. By "banging" on a program, they find bugs and report them back to the programmers, who fix them. Good testers are vital for making a solid piece of software. They know what the program is supposed to do, and make sure that the programmers get it right.

In this structure, notice that the programmers are the only ones who deal with the code of the program. Testers audit expected features, not unexpected ones. Management is happy as long as the program does what it is supposed to. And usually different parts of a program are divided among several people, so even other programmers don't look at each

other's code. If a programmer adds a hidden feature, chances are that neither testers nor management will notice it. And if it isn't caught by fellow programmers, it will go right to the public.

A time-delay is one technique used to hide an Easter egg. A product may behave completely normally until a certain date when the Easter egg becomes active. The testers never notice it, unless they happen to find it on that particular date. Or sometimes an egg can only become active after a certain date. A programmer could, for example, have the egg become active two weeks after it has been released to the public. Nobody would know about it until it's too late.

The only time many Easter eggs are caught and removed is when new programmers are assigned to change or update the project. The new programmers will go through the existing code extensively, and may stumble upon this strange extra feature.

> The only time many Easter eggs are caught and removed is when new programmers are assigned to change or update the project.

Very rarely do managers allow Easter eggs to remain in a product after they find out about them. After all, every bit of code makes a program bigger and uses more memory. I know I wouldn't want to be the manager who gets asked, "Why is our program twenty percent slower than our competitor's?" Granted, Easter eggs usually aren't processing hogs, but there are exceptions. Besides, in this extremely competitive marketplace, every little bit of extra speed helps.

When an Easter egg makes it to the store shelves and gets discovered, word of it will probably get back to the managers. Then, of course, they will try to remove it for the next version. That is why Easter eggs are almost always specific to a certain version of a product. For instance, Windows NT 3.51 doesn't have the same Easter eggs as Windows NT 4.0. When trying to get an egg to activate, always make sure you have the right version of the program or it probably won't work.

Why Easter Eggs Are Created

Now that we are clear on what Easter eggs are, we can ask the question: Why do they exist, especially in such vast quantities? Some of them take days, even weeks of effort that could be better spent improving the product or going to parties and being social (something EVERY coder should do a little more often). What possesses programmers to invest so much time and effort for these things that seem little more than inside jokes?

To get answers to these questions, we need to probe deeply, deep into the minds of typical programmers, down to their base animal nature, to what motivates them at the lowest level. Personally, the idea of going that deep into the mind of someone who spends ten hours a day staring at a computer screen gives me the willies. So I called in a professional to tackle this daunting task.

Dr. Stefan Broffenstuffel is one of the most famous, eminent, and practiced[1] psychologists in the world, having treated hundreds of patients in the software industry. I was lucky enough to gain an interview with him, and he provided great insights into the root causes of Easter eggs. His comments and information from developers themselves paint an accurate and intriguing picture of how Easter eggs are born.

Recognition

"Recognition and fame are extremely common motivators for creating Easter eggs" Dr. Broffenstuffel says,

"Putting" a nifty trick in a major piece of software and getting away with it has definite fame potential. It demonstrates superior ability as a programmer.

Creating the trick is clever, but sneaking it by management is a step above.

It shows individuality, boldness and creativity; maybe even some style and class. When this

> ### Dr. Stefan Broffenstuffel on Recognition
>
> " Every human craves personal recognition. It is a basic human need. Recognition by others affirms our sense of importance and self in the world. Without recognition for our accomplishments, we would be unhappy and unlikely to ever put forth the extra effort. People admire movie stars for their fame, the name in lights, the magazine cover, not the money. Programmers take immense pride in their creations, and need individual affirmation of their abilities. We all need to be told we are important as individuals, not just as part of a large conglomerate. "

---

[1] *And completely fictitious*

coder is sitting in a trendy Internet Bar (they're popping up everywhere now) and flirting with someone, he could throw out the line, "Hey baby, wanna come back to my place and see my Easter egg?" It would probably get him slapped, but you never know.

Another kind of recognition common to Easter eggs is a list of credits. Credits come up somewhere in most software, and if they aren't there by design, they are often included as an Easter egg. Usually all of the project developers are creatively listed. A perfect example of this kind of Easter egg is in Windows 95.

After a series of simple steps (detailed later in this book), a scene of a cloudy sky appears. The programmers names flow in and out of the clouds while music plays in the background. These kinds of eggs tell who exactly worked on the project hidden under the company name.

By showing off the egg and showing off his role in the product, the programmer gets recognition. The goal of the Easter egg is to associate one's name with an impressive piece of software. In today's corporate world, this is not easy. In a modern software company, a product has a large development group and while people put in tons of effort individually, it may not be very visible in the final release.

Software, unlike other published material, tends to emphasize the company behind it instead of the individuals. But the individuals are there and they rightfully deserve credit for the time and effort they spend on your software.

Nostalgia

Do you remember some things from your youth that seem totally awesome when you think back to them, but wouldn't impress you nearly as much now?

I've certainly got my list. I saw *Raiders of the Lost Ark* when I was very little, and the final scene where the Nazis' faces melted scared me half to death. I saw it again recently and the movie was entertaining, but I wasn't scared or repulsed in the least, but to this day I think of it as a "scary" movie.

> ### Dr. Stefan Broffenstuffel on Nostalgia
>
> " Events in our childhood effect us for the rest of our lives. They are burned into our minds while we are young and still very impressionable. A simple offhand remark to a child may be remembered for his entire life. Combined with the psychological desire to return to the womb, nostalgia for childhood and childhood events can become a powerful force in a programmer's psyche. "

Another movie example is *Tron*, which was *sooo* cool when I was a kid. However, I see it today in a more balanced perspective; the plot wasn't very good and the whole movie was kind of cheesy, but to me it will always have this aura of greatness from seeing it as a child.

Everybody has things they are nostalgic about: Star Wars, Star Trek, the Rubik's Cube, early video games, classic television shows, etc. All you need to do is take a look at the current "retro" fashion trend and the movies to see the power of nostalgia.

What Easter Eggs Are

There have been a slew of movies based on old TV shows: *The Brady Bunch Movie*, *The Flintstones*, *The Addams Family*, and others have all been popular in Hollywood recently. Everybody has their own nostalgic memories, and programmers are no exception.

Pong was the first commercial video arcade game. In case you've never seen it, it consisted of two "paddles" (which you could move from side to side) and a "ball" that bounced between them. The object was to bounce the ball past the opponent's paddle. All in all, it was a pretty simple game, which spawned variations throughout the development of computers, including Breakout, Arkanoid, and others.

Using advances in programming technology, writing Pong today is a fairly simple task that an experienced programmer can do in a day or two. But the nostalgia factor is immense. There are many applications and games that have Pong built in as an Easter egg.

Frank Filipanits is an audio DSP engineer who wrote plugins for a professional-grade audio system, Digidesign Pro Tools. He wrote an Easter egg into each plugin he developed, and here is what he said about his version of Pong.

My second project was the Procrastinator, a very long delay that I cranked out in a weekend on a whim—someone demoed it at a trade show the next weekend, and a product was born. Of course I had to outdo my last performance, but what to do? Isn't it obvious? Pong, my good man, PONG!

Yes, that's right—hold down shift-control as you open the 16-bit version of the plugin and you get a fully functional, fully playable pong game at the bottom of the window. I think it took me just as long to program the game as the product itself. It actually came in very handy though, at one trade show when I finished setup early and had an hour to kill...

The moral? Don't be surprised if you see a familiar old TV face or hear some early 'eighties music in your next word processor. Everyone has fond memories and eggs let programmers share theirs.

Humor

A shared sense of humor forms one of the closest bonds between two individuals. Picture all of your best friends in your mind. I bet every one of them shares a very similar sense of humor. People get along just fine without a common sense of humor, but shared humor can turn acquaintances into good friends.

When we crack a joke, we are trying to reach the common sense of humor in other people. We are trying to reach out and make a very personal connection.

> ### Dr. Stefan Broffenstuffel on Humor
>
> " Perhaps the single thing that distinguishes humans from all other animals on earth is our sense of humor. To this day, the definition of 'funny' still eludes us. We can't put a finger on it, but it is there. What's more, we all have senses of humor, and they are all unique. To appeal to the sense of humor in someone else is the ultimate in personal compatibility. If you can laugh together, everything else is easier. "

The same is true for programmers and their senses of humor. They want to reach out and connect with their peers' senses of humor, and a great way to do this is through an Easter egg. They think of funny things, and throw them into whatever they are working on at the time. Sometimes the humor is an inside joke, and other times it is aimed at a more general audience.

Many "Programmer Credits" Easter eggs include inside jokes. For example, if you find the list of developers for Netscape 3.0, each has a funny nickname. You can tell by looking that the names are meant as jokes, but as an outsider, you really don't know where they come from or why people got their nicknames. Only the people inside the company would know, and that is the target audience of the egg.

Some jokes, however, are aimed at a more general audience. Frank Filipanits, the audio DSP engineer mentioned previously, put a couple of eggs in his plugins that were solely based on popular humor. In one audio plugin, he embedded an animation of Beavis (from the TV show "Beavis and Butthead") "rocking out," swinging his head up and down to the music. He also embedded a joke based on the movie "The Net" in another plugin. Here, he tells it in his own words.

The *coup de gras* was my last project, DINR TDM, a noise reduction unit. I was working on it when *The Net* came out, and—inspired by the movie—I decided to have a little fun. Unfortunately, no one saw the movie, so it has a little less impact than I'd hoped. Part of the movie is about this virus infecting everyone's machines and this evil Microsoftian empire trying to subvert everyone's security mechanisms. Whatever.

The hook, though, is a little 'pi' symbol, that, when shift-control-clicked takes you to this 'praetorian' system and gives access to computers around the world. So I added my own little pi symbol to my DINR user interface. It doesn't grant you access to White Sands, but it **does** launch Netscape (if available) and brings up a web page off my home tree.

The kicker is that the pi symbol sat in the UI from early development all the way through ship (six or more months) and only one person ever asked me what it was. Once it shipped, more people were let in on the secret. . .

Humorous examples abound. In the game Duke Nukem 3D, the characters appear with different clothes on special holidays such as Halloween and Christmas. In windows NT 3.51, you can bring up a list of the programmers' favorite beers. Microsoft Excel has the "Hall of Tortured Souls," which must be seen to be believed. Jokes abound, and as long as there are programmers, they will continue to try to make us laugh.

Revenge

I don't see a whole lot of computer programmers turning into serial killers on the news. Generally, they're a pretty laid back lot who have got their heads screwed on straight. But programmers have feelings too, and when they are hurt, thoughts of vengeance cross their minds. Thankfully, their outlets for frustration are usually benign, and sometimes come in the form of Easter eggs.

A programmer's sense of pride is his or her most vulnerable spot. Telling a programmer the software into which they have put a sizable chunk of their life is bad is like telling a skilled carpenter that the house he just built is ugly.

Programmers, like other skilled craftsman, can get defensive about their work. A perfect example of a "revenge" Easter egg is in Microsoft Excel 4.0 for Windows. The Easter egg it contains shows an animation of the Excel logo squashing a spreadsheet competitor's "bugs" which are crawling around the screen.

Dr. Stefan Broffenstuffel on Revenge

" Vengeance is a strong and powerful motivater. It is very interesting because it mixes emotion and logic, where emotion takes logic too far. In a revenge situation, one party feels that it has been wronged by another party. It may be true, but the emotional force of revenge can carry away all logic and leave nothing behind except a seething desire to damage or injure the source of the injustice. "

Someone in the Excel group must have felt threatened by this competitor. Maybe they were beating Excel in some key markets. I don't know. But the egg is a clear slam on this competitor, and smacks of revenge. The next time you see an egg that puts down a competitor, you can bet that there is some personal revenge factor behind it. I wouldn't be surprised to see a whole lot of Microsoft vs. Netscape eggs in the near future.

Everyone is different

It is impossible to cover every possible reason for Easter eggs, but recognition, nostalgia, humor, and revenge make up a lot of the motivations out there. The different sources of inspiration for eggs are only constrained by human imagination. I've never seen a marriage proposal carried out through an Easter egg, but who is to say it will never happen? For all we know, someone could use an Easter egg to initiate a presidential campaign. All we can do is keep our eyes open and see what those wacky programmers think of next.

The Inside Scoop

Chapter

3

Chapter 3

The Inside Scoop

If you were writing a program, what Easter egg would you put in it? Where would you put it? Would it be something personal, like an office joke, or would it be something everyone could understand? Would your manager mind? Would you even tell your manager about it? Would you get away with it?

These are questions every programmer has to deal with when making an Easter egg. Of course, every person answers these questions differently. That's why there is such a variety of Easter eggs out there. We could sit and speculate over a programmer's motivation for hiding a picture of a can of Spam inside a virus protection program, but for all we really know it could just be the ravages of a deluded mind.

> To really get the inside scoop on an Easter egg we need to talk to the programmers themselves.

3 *The Inside Scoop*

To really get the inside scoop on an Easter egg we need to talk to the programmers themselves. Then we can find out what was really going on inside her or his head when s/he decided to get a creative in an otherwise straightforward program.

This chapter focuses on the causes, motivation and background of specific Easter eggs from the programmers' perspectives. It also includes related stories and follow-ups to see what happened once the product was released. You'll find out what tricks programmers use to put eggs into their software, as well as what management had to say about them. You can activate all of these eggs if you have the right software to see them yourself. Chances are, once you know the story behind these eggs, you'll find them even more amusing.

One more special bonus: also in this chapter is the complete story of an Easter egg that never made it to the release. It comes with screen shots and details of what happened to cause its removal. From this one example, you can imagine the thousands of Easter eggs that never quite made it, and appreciate even more the ones that did.

Along the way, the programmers' actual words have been preserved, with comments added in brackets ([ ]) when some especially arcane phrases appear.

PCBoard
From Stan Paulsen

Here is a great example of an Easter egg that resulted from code being forgotten and accidentally shipped in the release of the software. PCBoard is a piece of software used to run a Bulletin Board System (BBS). If you have a modem, you can dial up the BBS and use its services, such as message boards and E-mail. If you've ever called up a BBS before, there's a good chance you connected to a PCBoard system. To allow a system administrator to extend the PCBoard software, PCBoard includes the PCBoard Programming Language. It allowed programmers to add functions to the built-in language, making them "intrinsic functions." Stan Paulsen describes one of these intrinsic functions that accidentally made it into the final release.

I started out on the PPL (PCBoard Programming Language) as my first project at Clark Development. I was the sole developer on the project. The Easter egg was added by the original author, Scott Robison, as an example of how to add an intrinsic function to the language. The function did nothing but print the names and positions of some of the key staff at Clark Development. It was added in PCBoard v.15.1.

Once the function, called 'BRAG,' was added it was forgotten. No one realized it had made it into a release until one of our customers found the BRAG token, while browsing the binaries [the program files], and asked us what it was. I updated it for a few releases until the CEO found out it was there and instructed me to remove it. It is difficult to remove an intrinsic function from a language once it has been added since it would break any programs that happen to be using it. So I was instructed to have BRAG display what was essentially an advertisement for the product. Since advertising to customers who had already purchased the product wasn't a real bright idea, I finally made BRAG a no-op [no operation is performed] in PCBoard version 15.22. Bummer.

See what happens when you don't clean up after yourself!

Shokwave Software From Rob Hafernik

Rob Hafernik is the president of Shokwave Software, a company that does custom programming for other companies. Usually this software stays internal to the company instead of being available on the shelf for anyone to buy. However, some of their work is public, and they have a tradition for putting great Easter eggs in their products.

Rob gives some insight into the underlying meaning of these eggs he's put into programs. They certainly are more understandable with some background.

Over the years, we (the group of programmers that now make up Shokwave Software) have implemented lots of Easter eggs (but in mostly vertical-market products, so few people have seen them). One of our best was in a product called SaberLAN Workstation that we did for Saber Software Corporation. Robert Thurman, the engineer on one section of the product, implemented an About box that was the standard—a picture with an OK button. The picture was Saber Software's standard one of a beehive (don't ask why, it was just their 'look.' Something to do with 'worker bees' or something). However, if you held down the 'B' key when you brought up the About box (something I'll bet NO ONE did by accident), the beehive picture had animated bees flying all over, accompanied by a buzzing sound. The cursor became the queen bee and the others would follow her around as you moved the cursor. Saber released the product without ever knowing about the About box.

Another product for the Saber folks had a long scrolling list of credits. Near the bottom, it said 'no bees were harmed in the making of this software.

Here's an egg of Rob's which I would be a little scared to write. Remember that Easter eggs are generally HIDDEN, so you shouldn't run into them by chance. It's a good thing, too, since this next egg would really freak me out!

Yet another time, we did one (for an anti-virus software package) where the About box was just a picture, but, before it was shown on the screen, the horizontal scan lines of the picture were scrambled up, so the picture was unrecognizable. In fact, it looked like junk, as if something had gone horribly wrong. After the program put this up, it waited a bit, then scrambled the picture a little less and showed it again. Then a little more less and so on and so on. The picture sort of came into focus over the course of a few seconds, the trick being that the user thought the program had crashed or something at the beginning.

Scary stuff! Maybe programmers just don't realize the havoc they are able to wreak on the end user sometimes. But at least this egg isn't truly destructive. I don't know what inspired this next egg, other than a deep love of blue suede shoes. It's pretty snazzy.

One of our eggs used Balloon Help, in a product we did for TechWorks called 'GraceLAN Network Manager.' You brought up the About box, then turned on balloon help. If you put the cursor right over the 'o' in the TechWorks logo, a balloon popped up that had a picture of Elvis, with the text 'Thank you very much.' Yes, Easter eggs are fun.

All of these eggs from the same person! Talk about dedication! I wonder if he ever got any real work done.

Roaster
From Chris Evans

Chris put a little egg in his software with entirely personal significance. This is very common, and without any explanation, you would be left shaking your head saying, "Huh?!?"

In Roaster, the first Macintosh development environment for Java, version DR1, if you do a text search for 'Haagh,' it will play a little song. 'Haagh' was a very short song my band played in high school. The song is about four seconds long.

Lots of people put in little eggs like this, so if you stumble across one, confusion is natural. Just accept that it's something personal for the programmer. Hey, maybe you'll like the little 'Haagh' song!

SimCopter
From Paul Pedriana

With some computer games, you may run into some odd occurrence and wonder if it is an actual Easter egg, or just a regular part of the game. It's often a tough call, and the only way to be really sure is to ask the programmer. Luckily, that's what I had the opportunity to do with Paul Pedriana, a programmer for SimCopter.

> If you use helicopter bambi bucket to pick up water to put out fires, and you pick up the water too close to boats, there's a small chance that you will pick up a diver and he will fall out of the bucket when you drop the water on the fire. This is in reference to the urban legend of the diver stuck in a tree after a forest fire.

I wonder if that legend is true or simply a myth. In any case, it's pretty funny to be included in a "simulation" style game. I asked him if this (and other) eggs in SimCopter were known by other developers and management. Here's what Paul had to say:

> "We usually make all Easter eggs known to the development team, so they are basically approved. We also document them for legal reasons."

This isn't always the case, but it certainly helps for liability reasons. I certainly wouldn't want to get sued over an Easter egg. Or even worse, have some new "feature" suddenly appear in the product that embarrasses the company and causes my stock in it to go down.

Treasure Quest From Adam Schaeffer

Adam is currently a senior at the University of Washington. I was lucky enough to talk to him personally about his experience with Easter eggs, and he gave me the inside scoop on a particular Easter egg from its conception all the way through its implementation. What makes this one so special is that it never made it to the released product. Here we get a rare glimpse of an Easter egg that never made it through the management barrier.

Adam was working for a small software company called "Soggy in Seattle." When I say small, I'm not kidding; they only had about 5 people, total. Using their combined skills and a lot of determination, however, they managed to produce a great game called "Treasure Quest." You can find this game today on the shelves of software stores everywhere, and it's actually become something of a cult classic among gamers.

3

The problem with Soggy in Seattle was that they had a great product, but they were too small to have the marketing clout needed to distribute and market the product successfully on a large scale. Their solution was to have a larger company, Sirius, market Treasure Quest. So far so good, right?

Wrong. As time went on, relations between Soggy in Seattle and Sirius started to strain. The employees of the smaller company felt their work was being absorbed into the larger company. Eventually, they began to fear that they wouldn't even get credit for producing this wonderful piece of software.

Enter the Easter egg. The Soggy in Seattle programmers wanted to make sure they were given proper credit when this game went to market. So why not put in some personal credits? This is exactly what they did. Each member of the company had his or her own screen with a portrait and a quote of their choosing. The access mechanism to make these eggs appear had something to do with the About box, similar to many other Easter eggs. So it looked as though the "little guy" was going to triumph after all, at least as far as proving who really wrote the software.

It was not meant to be, however. The folks at Sirius wanted to port the game to other operating systems, such as both Macintosh and the PC. This gave them a reason to go digging through all of the code, and they found the Easter eggs. Naturally, they wanted them removed and had their way. So today, the Treasure Quest you find in stores remains sadly eggless. However, here are the screen shots of what you would have seen:

Summary

I hope you have enjoyed this romp through the innards of a few particular Easter eggs. It's nice to get a guided tour of the background and consequences of each Easter egg. Just think, there's a special story behind every egg just waiting to be told. With any luck, you'll get to hear it straight from the source. If you find an Easter egg, send some E-mail to the company. Maybe you can get in touch with the original programmer, or at least find out the story behind the Easter egg.

The Dark Side Of Easter Eggs

Chapter

4

Chapter 4

The Dark Side Of Easter Eggs

Easter eggs are great fun. Everyone enjoys Elvis leaping out of their personal accounting package, right? And it's hard to imagine a list of the programmers' names having an adverse effect on a product (other than decreasing your personal productivity because you pop the egg up to show all your friends). Easter eggs aren't malicious and provide hours of enjoyment for everyone, so what's the problem? Why do so many get stopped by management? What harm could they possibly do?

But Easter eggs do have a dark side. While I'm sure programmers don't intend any harm, putting eggs in products can have dire consequences.

> But Easter eggs do have a dark side...putting eggs in products can have dire consequences.

Valuable programming time can be wasted in programming these gadgets. Easter eggs are often untested and can cause all sorts of unintentional conflicts with the software. An errant programmer could unknowingly put something in an Easter egg that gets his company into big legal trouble.

These complex issues will be explained in greater detail with real life examples, but they should not deter you from enjoying existing eggs. In fact, knowing why they aren't very common makes the ones we have more valuable.

Wasted Time

Every hour a programmer puts into an Easter egg is an hour he or she could be enhancing product features, fixing bugs or performing further tests. Granted, this is an oversimplification. Sometimes programmers will put the extra effort in during their off hours or work on an egg only when there is nothing else they could be doing for the project. But in the vast majority of cases, a programmer creates the egg on company time.

"So what!" you say? Well, let's take a look at what this can really mean. "Bob" is a fictitious programmer working for NiftyWare Software. Let's say that Bob, over the course of a few months, spends a total of 40 hours of company time on a really cool Easter egg. That's a total of a whole work week for Bob. With programmers' salaries today, that could easily amount to between 500 and 1000 dollars worth of work. This money is of course factored into the development cost of the product (not to mention the cost of office space, heating, lighting, etc.). The buyers of the software naturally have to foot the bill, one way or another.

But this extra thousand dollars or so is really just a drop in the bucket when compared to the total cost of the software. The REAL damage is the prolonging of development time. In today's fast-paced computer market every day counts. If a piece of software can be shipped a week earlier, then it could mean a tremendous gain for the company. Maybe if Bob had put that work week into fixing bugs, the software could have shipped a week earlier—a distinct advantage over the competitors.

> "Wasted time" on Easter eggs might seem trivial, but for the bigger ones, it can be significant.

And if the egg is caught and removed, then the time and money truly have been wasted on an item that won't even make it out the door.

"Wasted time" on Easter eggs might seem trivial, but for the bigger ones, it can be significant. Every moment is precious in the exploding software marketplace, and time is one of the most expensive things to waste.

Wasted Space And Efficiency

Every line of code written to make an Easter egg takes up space. An egg might use a very small amount of space, but it still uses space; a program would definitely be smaller without the egg inside. For many programs, this isn't really a problem since the eggs are so simple. However, when large, complex Easter eggs are written, the size of the application can increase dramatically. Since smaller size is more desirable for all programs, this extra weight is a bad thing.

The worst consumers of extra space are large graphics. Even small graphics are never small files. When large or detailed pictures are added into an Easter egg, they can greatly increase the size of a program. To encode a picture, the data for every pixel must be stored somewhere. If the Easter egg involves an animated movie, watch out! That's a massive chunk of extra data, since each frame of the movie has to be stored somewhere within the program.

Losses in speed and efficiency can also be a problem, although this is rare in practice. If part of the Easter egg code is frequently running, it can slow down the running time for the useful parts of the application. For example, say an Easter egg checks for a certain keypress every millisecond. That means that an extra command is executed 1000 times every second. Depending on the speed of the computer, this extra effort could be costly and make the overall program run much slower.

It's true that most Easter eggs are pretty lean and mean and don't waste much space or efficiency. However, there are some notable exceptions, and programmers should always keep an eye out for these trade-offs when they write their Easter eggs.

Unwanted Side Effects

Since Easter eggs are outside of the main stream of software development, they aren't usually tested as thoroughly as regular program features. This may not be a problem when the eggs are simple, but in complex software side effects are definitely possible. Maybe under certain situations, the Easter egg will cause the software to crash, or even worse—crash your entire system. Maybe it will corrupt some of your data, making it unusable. No doubt the programmers never intended these side effects, but there is no way they could test their eggs under all possible conditions.

Ken Demarest, the lead programmer of the famous game Ultima VII, had this to say about Easter eggs and cheat codes:

"People spend an average of 150 hours finishing a game like Ultima. Could you please mention that if they use any cheats they're putting their game at risk? If you've used a cheat, you MIGHT HAVE made the game unwinnable, or even corrupt. Why? Because the cheats never get playtested, and anything that doesn't go through QA [Quality Assurance] can corrupt your game. I'm just trying to save somebody out there 150 hours of frustration."

Most small Easter eggs are unlikely to have side effects, but it's not unlikely in large ones. Also, the more complex the software itself, the more likely it is that a small change can produce unpredicted results.

> Most small Easter eggs are unlikely to have side effects, but it's not unlikely in large ones.

Ultima VII is a vastly complex game, and using cheats to alter it unexpectedly can lead to terrible consequences for the player. The moral is: You can never be sure how "harmless" an Easter egg might be, so use caution.

Debugging Mechanisms

While a program is being written and tested, it is common for the developer to insert extra code and controls as temporary tests. While great for testing, this code should be removed for the release version of the software. What happens when this code is forgotten and makes it into the release? Well, my friend, you just might have an Easter egg on your hands.

In some software, these hidden debugging features can be very amusing as Easter eggs for their strange behavior and ability to do bizarre things to a program.

But keep in mind that this code was never meant to be shipped. In all likelihood, it was forgotten from long ago. It might not even work anymore, or it might do destructive things to your data or the program. Beware of secret Debug Menus. They may be dangerous relics of a bygone software version.

Public Controversy

Occasionally, a programmer will include an egg that stirs up controversy or gets the company into trouble. This not only hurts the company and their software, but the developer might suffer repercussions. Legal action has been known to result from developers inserting other companies' logos somewhere in their Easter eggs. Naturally, no company wants to get sued, especially for something so easily avoidable. That's why eggs like this usually get squashed by management right away.

Another serious case arises when a programmer expresses personal feelings about a controversial subject. It can cause embarrassment to the company and punishment for the employee. Paul Pedriana, one of the core programmers of Maxis' "SimCopter," shared this story:

> "There is a sequence introduced by a gay programmer on the team where on rare occasions, when you complete the final level, men in bikinis come out and try to kiss you unless you can run back into your helicopter and take off before they get to you. Also, on 8/22, 9/30, or Friday the 13th, wacky things happen in the game, such as there are dozens of Elvis impersonators all over the place. This egg was not told to management and was considered distasteful, and the programmer was fired about three weeks ago."

The *New York Times* covered the same Easter Egg in a full story printed on Decemeber 8, 1996.

Summary

Not everything about Easter eggs is positive. They definitely carry their own baggage with them in the form of risks and waste.

Overall, though, Easter eggs are relatively harmless and should be enjoyed for their entertainment value. We've all run into software bugs that have done worse things than any Easter egg will. Treat them as you would any piece of "beta" software. Use caution, but don't be too afraid of bad consequences. Easter eggs are labors of love, and may have even gotten more personal attention from the developers than the actual product.

The Past And Future Of Easter Eggs

Chapter

5

Chapter 5

The Past And Future Of Easter Eggs

Easter eggs have been around probably since the dawn of computers. Every programmer puts a little personality into what they create, and some imbue more "personality" into their code than others. As long as computers have humans behind their operation, Easter-egg-like behavior will always be around.

What did the first Easter eggs look like? How common were they? What is different about today's Easter eggs? What is likely to become of these rogue functions in the future? In this chapter I will cover all the history I have been able to gather about Easter eggs, explain the present state of the field and make predictions about the future. Remember, Easter eggs don't exactly leave a paper trail, so what we know is bound to be incomplete. Yet sleuths everywhere have been able to discover enough to sketch out a rough history of Easter eggs and their development.

In The Beginning . . .

The first computers appeared in the late 1940s. They were behemoths, the size of several rooms. They had vacuum tubes to do their computations and were enormously slow by today's standards. Yet, it was a beginning. There weren't any hard drives and very little "memory." Data was stored on punch cards, which were fed into the machine. A "user interface" was practically non-existent.

Programming these original mainframes was no easy task. If you wanted something done, you hired a specialist who wrote your program from start to finish. There was no compatibility. If you needed something to run on another type of computer, you had to hire another specialist to rewrite it. Nobody had any large-scale software development. Each program was written by one person, or at most a few people.

I don't know of any particular Easter eggs from that era, but I can make a good guess what it was like, based on programmers today. Put yourself in one of those programmers' shoes. You had total control over the entire project. Sure, you had to meet the customer's needs, but if you threw some extra code in, they wouldn't know the difference. In fact, *nobody* would be the wiser, since your code wasn't going to be used on any other machines.

With this amount of control, it would be hard to resist throwing some personal stuff into your code. It might be as simple as extra commands left in the code when you were debugging. Why bother cleaning up your code when no one else would ever mess with it? Remember too, you didn't have a lot of extra computing power to spare. Good programs were efficient programs, plain and simple.

The most likely results of all this were leftover functions that never got cleaned up. Since the programs were run only according to specifications, the leftovers were never discovered. In today's world, they would be considered Easter eggs, but back then they would just be considered undesirable extra code.

Multi-user systems

As computers started getting larger and more complex (and using transistors instead of vacuum tubes), a new computing model began to emerge. A single computer had enough power to be shared among several users. The sixties and seventies made up the age of multi-user, time-shared systems. Under this model, a single computer would be connected to several terminals. A user could sit at each terminal and do work on the computer, and the computer would give each terminal a little slice of it's computing time. If the computer was fast enough, none of the users would even notice a delay and it would seem as though they had the computer all to themselves. A time-sharing computer system utilized the expensive computer resources more efficiently, allowing more work to get done in less time.

Computers also began to reap the benefits of the manufacturing process and economies of scale. No longer did each mainframe have to be custom built for the customer. IBM and others now produced standard mainframe and minicomputer models which were produced in larger quantities. Now you could write a program for one computer and other people in the world might have the same exact computer capable of also running your code. Computers were still expensive, but no longer in the millions of dollars range, as during the fifties. More and more institutions and large companies were buying computers.

To handle the increased standardization and complexity of the computer industry, the first true *operating systems* were developed. UNIX rose to power during this period because it was a powerful, multi-user operating system that could run on lots of different computers. Code written for a certain brand of UNIX could be ported not only to all the other machines that matched yours, but to all the machines running UNIX! For the first time, software distribution started to become important.

> What did all these changes do for Easter eggs? Easter eggs had to change with the times, of course.

What did all these changes do for Easter eggs? Easter eggs had to change with the times, of course. Since software written by one single person might be spread and run on all sorts of different systems, the likelihood of discovery increased greatly. If you distributed the source code to your program, as was necessary in some cases, any amateur hacker or coder could root through it and find your Easter eggs. It was hard to keep a secret in these types of systems, and computing power was still relatively expensive. I'm sure any Easter egg that consumed a lot of computing resources was heavily frowned upon within the computing community. The methods of displaying anything to the user were still primitive and primarily text-based. All of these influences discouraged Easter eggs in software.

Every coin has a flip side, however. Wider distribution of software also meant more people were running what you wrote. If you wanted to put something funny in your program, you now had an audience. Everyone wants a little fame and recognition, and throwing a little joke in your program is a harmless way to get it.

The net effect is that Easter eggs finally emerged as a distinct arena. They were probably still as frequent as before, but their nature had changed. No longer were they accidental relics of sloppy programming, but most of them were

> The era of primitive Easter eggs had begun.

put in there on purpose. Constrained by a primitive user interface, they manifested themselves as little humorous blurbs, maybe as a response to some particular user input. Perhaps if you ran a program with a certain command line parameter, it would spit a funny error message back. The era of primitive Easter eggs had begun.

The Personal Computer Emerges

Two key events founded the Personal Computer revolution. One was Intel's development of the first microprocessor. The other was Steve Jobs inventing the Apple personal computer. What made these events so crucial is that they created a means of personalizing computing power and making it affordable to an average citizen. You no longer had to be a huge company or a governmental institution to afford a computer. You could go to a local store and buy one for your own personal use.

Talk about a revolution! The Apple II, the IBM PC, the Commodore 64, the TI-99, and a slew of other personal computer products appeared. We had affordable electronic media, like magnetic tapes and floppy disks—no more punch cards! Now computers used transistor memory known as RAM. People started buying computers for offices, for their homes, and even for their children to play with.

With Personal Computers, software had enormous distribution potential. If you wrote a Commodore 64 program, you could package it up, market it and sell it at every local computer store. If you wanted to give something to a friend, you just had to trade floppies. Heck, you didn't even have to leave your house. A modem would let you call your friend's computer over the phone and transfer data that way.

With millions of personal computers out there, you also had millions of amateur hackers and programmers. I'm a child of this generation; I was writing code for the Apple II when I was in elementary school. I know hundreds of people who got initiated into the world of programming through their Commodore 64. And the more programmers there are, the more Easter eggs, right?

With a huge distribution network, an Easter egg is likely to get a huge viewing audience. An Easter egg will only be using the resources of a single person's computer, so a complex task won't take computing power away from other users, as it would in a time-sharing system.

> With a huge distribution network, an Easter egg is likely to get a huge viewing audience.

Another benefit is that programs could now be shipped as "object code" only. That meant that the programmer's source code wasn't available to the public and wasn't open to wide criticism or critique (or hacking). The chance of getting an actual hidden feature through to the public was dramatically increased.

Of course, negative factors weighed against Easter egg development, also. As computers became more widespread and powerful, the programs became more complex and robust. This often required teams of programmers, instead of a lone coder. In a team environment, discovery of an Easter egg by other team members is very likely, so getting an egg into a complex project usually requires approval by the entire team.

> The net result
> on Easter eggs
> during the
> 'eighties was
> positive
> overall.

The net result on Easter eggs during the 'eighties was positive overall. With graphics now possible, the eggs could be larger and more graphically interesting. A large market and good distribution for both commercial and independent software led to a lot of small Easter eggs in many products. While eggs in large commercial products were still relatively uncommon, the huge base of independent and amateur programmers provided a large injection of personal taste and creativity to the market, resulting in many Easter eggs in smaller products. Easter eggs thrive on programmer independence and there was no better time for the independent programmer than this period.

The GUI And The Internet

Ten years ago, it would have been hard to imagine a PC user who didn't have to memorize tons of cryptic commands just to get a little work done. Graphics were for games, not everyday use. Lots of PC users didn't even own a mouse, and it went unused by many who did.

Personal computers were isolated machines, separated almost entirely from other machines, except in the case of big businesses who might have a local area network.

The nineties have changed the computing paradigm yet again, and two key components, the Graphical User Interface (GUI) and the Internet, have taken computers beyond mere affordability and into mainstream American life.

The GUI emerges

Microsoft's release of Windows 3.0 in the early 1990s gave PC users the opportunity for a true graphical user interface, like Apple's Macintosh already had. Because PC's generally had more raw power for the money than their Macintosh counterparts, the addition of a GUI to the PC co-opted Apple's main advantage, and a new generation of computer users were opting for PCs in droves.

Evolving their GUI interface and operating system over time, Microsoft produced Windows 3.1, Windows for Workgroups, Windows 95 and Windows NT. Today over 80 percent of computers run a Microsoft operating system, and many people can't conceive of any other way to use a computer than pointing and clicking on graphics and buttons.

The rise of the GUI has led to dramatic changes in how people view computers. First of all, the use of graphics in all forms is now commonplace. When you are writing a paper, you can easily insert pictures into your text and preview the finished product. Buttons and menus have replaced the old cryptic text commands. Audio and video can be blended with amazing quality and you can even watch television on your PC if you want to.

Overall, people view computers and software as being more friendly and helpful. The PC is no longer thought of as a "tool," as in the past, but instead as an "environment" to spend time in, both for work and for leisure.

Growth of the Internet

Couple the GUI with the Internet and things *really* change. Before the Internet, few people owned modems. Those who did would usually only use them to connect to a few other individuals or local bulletin board systems (BBSs) to post messages or transfer files. People didn't own modems unless they had a real need for them or were hard-core compuphiles. Enter the Internet.

The worldwide computer network we know today as the Internet had it's beginnings in the sixties. During the height of the Cold War, the US government wanted a nationwide control network that could survive a nuclear war.

The task of solving this problem was given to the Advanced Research Projects Agency (ARPA). Their solution was the experimental ARPANET, which went online in December, 1969, connecting four universities:

- University of California at Los Angeles (UCLA)
- UC at Santa Barbara
- Stanford Research Institute (SRI)
- University of Utah

The growth was rapid, with many other governmental and university institutions joining within the first few years. By the late 1970s, the National Science Foundation (NSF) realized the enormous impact the ARPANET was having and decided to design a new successor that would be open to all university research groups.

The resulting NSFNET went online in 1984, and this network also connected to ARPANET. It was an instant success and was overloaded from the start. By the mid '80s people began viewing the collection of networks of ARPANET, NSFNET and others as a collective Internet, and later the Internet (with a capital I). In 1990 it had 3000 networks and 200,000 computers. By 1992 it connected one million computers. By 1995 it had grown to tens of millions of users and the size doubles approximately every year.

> By 1995 it had grown to tens of millions of users and the size doubles approximately every year.

Connecting to a network this size holds immense benefits for a user. He can send electronic mail on this network, which is rapidly becoming a favored means of communication. He can read news and message groups, as well as post to them. He can transfer files to and from his home machine from anywhere in the world. He can remotely log into other machines and get work done from home or on the road. He can pop up a web browser and hop from graphical site to graphical site in search of any information that suits his fancy. These combined benefits make connecting to the Internet very attractive and everyday more people jump on the bandwagon. Modems are now standard equipment and a computer user without an E-mail address is becoming rarer and rarer.

GUI and Internet impacts on Easter Eggs

I'm sure you're saying, "Thanks for the history lesson, but what does this have to do with Easter eggs?" it has everything to do with Easter eggs! The GUI and the Internet are mainly responsible for the amazing complexity and awareness that Easter eggs enjoy today. Without them, you wouldn't even be reading this book.

> The effects of the GUI on Easter eggs are pretty obvious.

The effects of the GUI on Easter eggs are pretty obvious. A GUI interface allows people to easily incorporate graphics, sound and animation into their products. All of the coolest Easter eggs that exist today have spiffy graphics or good music. Now programmers have a means of presenting s o m e t h i n gvisual, instead of just text. You know what they say: a picture is worth a thousand words. Try describing a funny photograph to your friends. No matter how hard you try, I bet it won't be as funny as one glance at the original picture. With a GUI interface, a programmer can become visually creative and become an artist instead of only a clever writer. A GUI interface also lets the user find and activate the egg easier. Heck, the GUI environment as a whole is very conducive to Easter eggs.

The positive effects of the Internet on Easter eggs may not be quite as obvious. Before, you were lucky to know a programmer personally who shared his Easter egg secrets with you. Maybe you even used a few of these to impress your friends. But without a widespread means of communicating this information rapidly to many people, it wouldn't get out very much. Maybe an article would be published in a magazine if an Easter egg was really big and was in a popular product, but for the most part eggs were found and then forgotten.

> The positive effects of the Internet on Easter eggs may not be quite as obvious.

The rise of the Internet provided a huge new communications medium for information of all kinds, including Easter egg knowledge. Now, using the Internet, someone who finds an egg can tell people all over the world instantly. Through the Internet, eggs in even the most obscure products can be catalogued and enjoyed by those who own those products. That's why I was able to start the Easter Egg Archive. It was easy and people from all over the world can now discover and post information about the eggs in their favorite products.

A side benefit of this democratizing of information is more fame for the programmers who manage to sneak Easter eggs into their products. Programmers have more incentive than ever to make their Easter eggs bigger, better and cooler. As any economist will tell you, competition leads to higher quality and bigger volume. That's why we have great Easter egg traditions, like in the Microsoft Excel group. Even small software companies are releasing products with Easter eggs that they know about and *want* you to find. As Easter eggs grow in popularity, I don't see their production slowing down any time soon.

Beyond 2000

We are living in a Golden Age for Easter eggs. Who knows what the future may bring? None of us knows for sure, but I'll make some educated guesses based on trends in the technology I see on the horizon. I'll even take a stab at the far future to catch a glimpse at what our grandchildren may see.

VRML and Virtual Worlds

The current language of the World Wide Web is HTML, which stands for HyperText Markup Language. Any pages you see on the Web are written in HTML. A new standard on the horizon is VRML, which stands for Virtual Reality Markup Language.

HTML describes objects on a page, while VRML describes objects in space. Look for Web browsers in the near future to support VRML and be aware of a growing number of VRML sites around the world.

Don't you think it would be just as easy to hide an Easter egg in a 3-D world as it is to hide an object in your own house? Maybe you will stop off at your favorite VRML Web site, lift up a lamp and activate some cool Easter egg.

VRML is the first step toward true Virtual Reality and Virtual Worlds, but true VR is still a ways off. Rapid progress is being made, however, and VR could be here sooner than any of us expect. Many fascinating new technologies are being developed at the Human Interface Technology lab at the University of Washington.

They are developing Retinal Imaging Goggles that project light directly onto your eye instead of onto a screen. This would let you retain your full field of vision and also be able to turn your head freely, visually panning the virtual environment. Amazing, but that's not all! They are also developing methods for simulating three dimensions on your PC screen and touch response to simulate the feel of real objects.

Through their work and the work of others around the world, Virtual Reality may not be "virtual" in ten or twenty years, and the opportunities for amazing new Easter eggs will multiply like holiday bunnies. How would you react if you pressed a secret button in a virtual world and the programmer materialized, shook your hand and then had an interactive conversation with you? It may not happen soon, but I wouldn't rule it out somewhere down the road.

Artificial Intelligence

Have you ever cursed at your computer for being such a dumb piece of junk? You know exactly what you want to do, but it just doesn't seem to be accommodating. Well, in the future that may change. Remember HAL from the movie 2001? Computers with artificial intelligence (AI) are not far away. Lots of research is being done in the field, both by academic institutions and businesses, with new breakthroughs being made all the time.

Within ten years I wouldn't be surprised if a standard operating system has artificial intelligence elements built in. Do you usually configure your software a certain way? Your PC could learn this and automatically do it for you the next time you install something. Are you frequently hunting down a certain function in a program? Your computer would figure it out and add a shortcut button on your toolbar. Even today's Microsoft Word has the beginnings of artificial intelligence in its AutoFormat capabilities. Soon, your computer may know what you want to do before you do.

I can think of some really interesting Easter eggs if AI is present in a PC. An Easter egg for one program might use AI to show you all the known Easter eggs in the other software you have installed on your PC. Artificial intelligence has the potential for any mischievous behavior, from hiding your folders to making your mouse act funny to dialing up to the Internet and connecting to a web site. It all depends on how far this field progresses and how much any single program can control the system AI. We certainly don't want any real HALs on our hands.

Distributed computing

With more and more people connecting to networks, distributed computing is gaining popularity again. Distributed computing is the ability to spread out the running of one program over several machines on a network, allowing it to run much faster than if you only had a single PC. Distributed computing not only allows for bigger eggs, but also the possibility of needing multiple programs to activate it. Maybe some future version of Microsoft Office will have an Easter egg that only appears when each of it's applications are being run at the same time from different machines on a distributed network.

Neural interfaces

Sometime in the far future, technology may advance far enough for a direct computer to human link. Try to imagine plugging *yourself* into a computer network. It has been envisioned by many science fiction authors and I see it as a distinct possibility in the far future. I hate to even speculate what Easter eggs might be in programs that deal with neural interfaces, but I'm sure they will be like nothing we can imagine today. With the entire range of human senses, thoughts, experiences and emotions at their disposal, the programmers of the future will be able to do amazing things. Maybe, as an Easter egg, you will get to *be* the programmer as he is writing the Easter egg. Whoa... that's straight out of an Escher drawing.

Summary

Easter eggs have certainly progressed over the years. They grew from unintentional near-bugs to simple jokes, into full fledged graphical programs. There are more known eggs being produced today than ever before, and they just keep getting more and more impressive. In the future we will see eggs we can't even conceive of from the vantage point of today. I have faith that eggs will continue to amaze and delight us in coming generations of technology.

Finding
Easter Eggs

Chapter

6

Chapter 6

Finding Easter Eggs

Easter eggs can't be too obvious. It takes all the fun out of them. Easter eggs carry a sense of wonder and secrecy, and every new discoverer feels he or she has found buried treasure. Easter eggs have to start out secret. Only over time, as discoverers tell friends, and friends in turn tell other friends, do these little treasures become public knowledge.

Since eggs are undocumented, people must spread this knowledge from person to person, and it would be impossible for every user of every product to hear about the eggs in their software. Even today the most popular and amazing Easter eggs are known only to a small fraction of the computing community, and that's what makes them special to the people who know about them.

> You certainly don't need to be a computer expert to find Easter eggs. In fact, you may not even need a computer.

You certainly don't need to be a computer expert to find Easter eggs yourself. In fact, you may not even need a computer. This chapter describes various techniques that you can use to discover Easter eggs on your own. It starts with methods for the novice computer user and ends with a few things that should only be attempted by people who regularly say phrases like, "an optimized L2 cache could reduce the bus bandwidth demands of fractal rendering." Not to worry, whatever your level of computer experience, you too can discover new Easter eggs and pass on their legacy.

The Easter Egg Archive

If you've got a computer hooked up to the Internet, then you can visit The Easter Egg Archive on the World Wide Web. Just get connected, fire up your favorite web browser and get to:

```
http://weber.u.washington.edu/
~davidnf/eggs/
```

... visit The Easter Egg Archive on the World Wide Web...
http://weber.u.washington.edu/~davidnf/eggs/

Remember though, everything on the net is subject to change. If the above address doesn't work, try searching for "Easter Egg Archive" on your favorite search engine, and it should point you to the new location.

The Easter Egg Archive is a site I started over a year and a half ago to gather and catalogue Easter egg knowledge. Since then I've accumulated and indexed hundreds thanks to egg hunters around the world, so check here first. It also has a list of "recent eggs" that all of you can post to when you discover a new Easter egg.

Brute Force

Are you over 6'4", weigh over 250 pounds, and have the affectionate nickname "Caveman?" Are you a member of a powerful Mafia crime family? Are you known for your The methods of "physical persuasion?" Do you have diplomatic immunity? If you answered "Yes" to any of these questions, brute force may be an option for you. Heck, it could work for anybody.

How does the brute force method work? It's very simple. With the proper type and amount of persuasion, even the most iron-willed programmer will divulge his Easter egg secrets. You don't even have to know what a computer is to carry this plan out. Here is the step-by-step procedure:

1. Find a programmer.

2. "Persuade" the programmer.

3. Walk away with Easter eggs.

For the "persuasion" step, stick to whatever you do best. Maybe you could offer "protection" in exchange for Easter eggs. Bribery has been known to work well. You would be amazed at how little effort it might actually take. In fact, the most successful method known is to just ask politely. Most of the time, they'll be more than happy to tell you, even if you aren't big and burly. A little polite conversation and a pleasant demeanor can take you a long way.

So get out there and find some programmers. If you just fire off an E-mail message to them asking about their personal or company Easter eggs, they may be very helpful. After all, Easter egg lovers have to stick together.

Personal Connections

How did you find out about your first Easter egg? Most people learn about them through their friends and co-workers. Word of mouth is a great medium for spreading this type of "secret" information, since many of us love to show off our knowledge. You don't even need to own your own computer to learn about Easter eggs this way. All you need are some friends or personal connections.

This is how most Easter egg information gets around. Someone finds a cool Easter egg and shows it off to their friends. Those friends show it to other friends, and eventually it becomes public information by being published, like in a magazine or this book.

If you're curious about new Easter eggs, ask your friends. They may have run across some new ones, and can pass their newly found knowledge on to you. Do you know any programmers personally? Ask them about their projects and see if they put any in their software. They probably won't mind giving the low-down on their latest Easter egg to a good friend. In fact, they may even give you a peek at it before the software is released.

Simple word of mouth is responsible for a great deal of the public Easter egg knowledge out there. Let's face it, some of the instructions to eggs are *so* bizarre that no one could have figured them out with random trial and error.

The programmers themselves want to show off their Easter eggs, so they tell a few friends. Knowing how well people tend to keep secrets, the knowledge slowly leaks from these friends and makes it out to the public eventually.

Don't underestimate the power of personal connections. You can get some really hot new Easter eggs this way. Who knows what your sister's husband's brother's plumber's cousin's teacher's ex-girlfriend put in her software?

> Don't underestimate the power of personal connections. You can get some really hot new Easter eggs this way.

6

Logos

Company or product logos are very easy to check, and they frequently have some sort of Easter egg hidden in them. Since an Easter egg usually is directly related to the software, it is often connected to the product or company logo. Some eggs are lists of programmer credits, and can often be found by somehow clicking on a logo and/or performing a special action. Browse around the software, and anywhere you see a logo, click on it. Click on different parts of it. Try to drag it across the screen. Yell at it. Make sure it gets plenty of sunlight. Take it out to a fancy restaurant. Let it play lead guitar in your band. Do anything you can think of to the logo. It may be hiding a special treat.

Logo Easter eggs are very common. Word 95 for Windows has a scrolling list of credits pop up when you type the word "blue," modify it in a few ways and then click on the Microsoft Word logo. The Windows 3.1 egg is linked to the Microsoft logo. Netscape and Lotus CC:Mail also have eggs directly linked to their logos. Check the catalogue of Easter eggs later in this book for explicit instructions on how to activate these eggs.

So the next time you boot up your hot new personal information manager program, click around on the logo and see what happens. It's easy to try and can yield very fruitful results.

Summary instructions

Find the product or company logo.

◆ Try clicking on it. Click on different parts of it, click on it with each of your mouse buttons and don't forget to try double-clicking.

◆ Try holding all combinations of the Ctrl, Alt, and Shift keys while clicking on it.

◆ Try clicking on the logo, holding the mouse button down, and dragging it to other locations on the screen. If the logo is set up as a drag-and-drop object, your cursor will change from the standard arrow to something else.

The "something else" depends on what operating system you are using and what set of icons you have installed. If the cursor changes, it is a HUGE clue that the logo might contain an Easter egg. Drag it around the screen and try to find a location that will "accept" the drag-and-drop object.

You will notice that the cursor is different when you drag the logo to an "accepting" spot than it is when you are dragging on the rest of the screen. If you find an "accepting" spot, let go of the mouse and see what happens. You've probably found your egg!

If all of these tests fail, then the logo is probably just a logo. Look around to see if the logo appears anywhere else in the program. If it does, repeat these tests on it there.

"About" Box

Most applications today have a "Help" menu. In this menu, there is almost always a selection "About this product" which you can select to get a screen full of information about that particular piece of software. Under normal circumstances, it contains a little blurb about the product version, some copyright information, and maybe the product or company logo. Potentially useful information if you're planning to call tech support or are wondering what version is installed. But it's not that fascinating, so users rarely visit this screen. A place users rarely visit? Ah!—the perfect place to hide an Easter egg!

It turns out that a large percentage of Easter eggs are hidden in the About box. Users rarely see it, and the About box is where users are looking for additional information about the product anyway. Why not stick a secret list of credits or a few jokes in there? Programmers do it all the time, and in fact most of Microsoft's Easter eggs are connected with the About box.

Give it a whirl with software you have on your system. Bring up the About box and try poking and clicking and typing weird key combinations. You've got nothing to lose, except maybe a little sanity if you keep it up for too long. Chances are, the programmers won't make it too hard to find, since they want people to see the eggs at some point. You may be surprised by what turns up.

Summary instructions

◆ Go to the "Help" menu.

◆ Select any menu items that start with "About." Most will have "About *product*" where *product* is the name of the software you are using.

◆ If there is a logo in the box that appears, then apply the logo tests from the previous section.

◆ If there are buttons in the box, click on them and see what happens. Try holding combinations of Ctrl, Alt, and Shift and clicking on the buttons. Try clicking on the buttons in different orders.

◆ Are there any other outstanding features in the box? Apply the logo tests from the previous section to them.

◆ If you have tried all of the above, but still don't find an Easter egg, then it's probably located somewhere else or requires some special input somewhere else to activate it. However, all is not lost. Take down any special information in the About box that might help you in the future. Special keywords or programmers' names might come in handy later.

♦ Are any email addresses listed? If so, you might try firing off an email asking about Easter eggs in the product. Even tech support might know about some and be happy to tell you.

Hot Keys

A "hot key" is a key combination that is used as a shortcut for a common operation. For example, in many applications Ctrl - S is the hot key for saving a file; it's easier than moving your hand off the keyboard, grabbing the mouse, going to the File menu and then selecting "Save." Most applications have hot keys built in for common functions, but a few have them built in for Easter eggs.

Try out all of the possible key combinations for a particular application. Hold Ctrl, Alt, and Shift (and Option on the Mac) and any combination thereof while pressing keys on the keyboard.

You may turn up an Easter egg. The Easter egg in the OS/2 operating system is activated this way.

WARNING

While trying all of these key combinations, make sure that you don't hit a hot key for a known destructive function, like "delete all files." While most modern apps are smart enough to prompt you before doing anything destructive, some may not prompt you. Just be careful when using this method and find any potentially destructive hot keys beforehand.

Summary instructions

◆ Make a list of all known hot keys for the program and also for the underlying operating system. You especially want to note all hot keys that do something destructive.

◆ Hold Ctrl and press all keys not on your list. Repeat while holding Alt, then while holding Shift. Repeat again with the combinations Ctrl - Alt, Ctrl - Shift, and Alt - Shift. Finally, repeat while holding down all three. Take note of any unexpected actions and what keys you pressed to activate them.

◆ Close down the program. Repeat the hot keys you found. If the action still happens, even without the program running, then you know it must be caused by another program or the operating system.

◆ Restart the program from scratch and test all hot keys that you found to be specific to that piece of software from step 3. If you can reproduce the behavior, double check the manuals and online help to make sure it's not a legitimate feature of the product. If not, you've found an Easter egg! Congratulations!

◆ Now to test the hot keys from step 3 that weren't due to that particular piece of software. Take note of what programs are running on your system. Close one of them down and repeat the hot keys in question. If an action isn't repeated, then you've found the suspect program. You may have inadvertently found an Easter egg in some other product! Repeat this step until all of the programs are closed.

◆ If you still have suspect hot keys even when all programs are closed, you may have found an Easter egg in the operating system itself. Again, check to make sure it's not a genuine feature before going off and telling all of your friends.

Key Words And Phrases

Ever since computer games have been on the market, programmers have used certain words and phrases to trigger special behavior. I remember an old game I played many years ago titled "Conquests of Camelot," by Sierra. In this game you played the role of King Arthur.

As the famous hero of legend, you went around the game having adventures and searching for the Holy Grail. The game was your standard adventure game; you went from place to place finding objects, having battles, and solving puzzles. However, in one room if you typed "ham and jam and spam a lot" a bunch of knights would come dancing across the screen in full armor like chorus line girls.

The reference, if you don't recognize it, is from the (in)famous British movie "Monty Python and the Holy Grail." In the movie, there was an entire scene where all the knights were singing and dancing around while making all sorts of rhymes with the word "Camelot." This little bit of pop culture fit in with the theme of Conquests of Camelot perfectly as an Easter egg.

The tradition of using key words and phrases for triggering Easter eggs carries on to applications. It isn't just for games anymore. Many Easter eggs are triggered by simply entering the right text in the right place.

One of the most popular eggs of this kind is the 3D Text screen saver for Windows NT. The screen saver lets you type in some text and it renders your words in three dimensions bouncing it all around the screen, twisting and turning.

They also hid some secrets in this screen saver. In version 3.51, if you type "I love NT" as the text, the screen saver will show the names of the programmers floating around in 3D. If you type in "beer" you will get the names of different beers floating around. When you enter "music" or "rock," a list of popular bands appears. This Easter egg must have become a tradition, because it was carried over into Windows NT version 4.0. In this latest version you can type "volcano" to get a list of mountains.

You too should try to find these Easter eggs based on trigger words. If there is any place in a program where you are asked to enter some text, or especially your name, try putting in special phrases. Sometimes the company or product name might be the trigger. Or it could be the name of one programmer.

Try anything you can think of relating to the product. Maybe a product has a running inside joke. Inside jokes build up easily in series of games and may do the same in sequential versions of applications. Try everything, and one of your choices could activate something special.

Common key phrases

The programmers names or nicknames

- ◆ The name of the product

- ◆ The product or company mascot—for example, Netscape's "Mozilla"

- ◆ An common acronym—for example, MSN is an acronym for The Microsoft Network; PDA is an acronym for Personal Digital Assistant

- ◆ A homonym (sounds the same) or play on words—for example, "X97:L97" is part of the activation for the Easter egg in Excel 97

- ◆ Names of famous people—OJ Simpson and Elvis are a couple of good examples

- ◆ Inside jokes within the company or product group

- ◆ Competitors and their products

- ◆ Catch phrases, like "Do you feel lucky, punk?"

Past History

The best predictor of future behavior is past behavior. Managers know this when they are trying to hire someone for a job. That's why they ask for a resume and check references. People who have done good work in the past will tend to do good work in the future. Habitual criminals are likely to repeat offenses. A judge knows that someone who has committed many crimes in the past is likely to commit future crimes, and will probably give a harsher sentence to a repeat offender than he would to a first time offender. Of course there are many exceptions to this rule, but history is a remarkably helpful predictor of the future.

History can also help you find new Easter eggs. Consider the recently released Microsoft Office 97. Microsoft not only has a long Easter egg tradition as a company, but Microsoft Excel in particular has a tradition of great Easter eggs.

Using past history as a guide, Easter egg hunters descended with wild abandon on the newly released Excel 97 to find the Easter egg that absolutely *had* to be there somewhere. Sure enough, within just a few days of its release, posts started coming in to the Easter Egg Archive describing how to activate the Easter egg in Excel 97.

The hunters were not disappointed either. Keeping with tradition, the egg was an amazing three dimensional landscape containing the programming credits. The speed at which Easter egg hunters around the world discovered the new egg was stunning. They also found eggs in Word and Powerpoint almost as fast. They could do this because they used clues based on eggs in previous versions of the software.

You can use history to help find eggs for yourself. Use the following checklist to help in finding clues to the location of Easter eggs.

◆ Has the company put out any other products with Easter eggs in them? If they have, it's very likely an Easter egg exists in this product. If not, then don't be too disappointed if you don't find any eggs. Some companies are much more "egg friendly" than others.

◆ Have there been any past versions of this product that contain Easter eggs? Every version of Microsoft Excel I've ever used contains an Easter egg of some sort, so future versions will most likely continue to have them.

◆ Where were eggs located of in previous versions of the software? In Windows NT, both versions 3.51 and 4.0 have Easter eggs hidden in the 3D Text screen saver. Search the locations of previous Easter eggs especially hard in any latest version that hits the market.

◆ Is there a theme to the previous Easter eggs? Maybe bees were prominent in all previous eggs. If they were, then probably the egg in this version has something to do with bees. It may just be some inside joke with the programming team, but nonetheless it is a pattern that can help in your search.

Think Like A Programmer

In the police force, detectives try to get inside the minds of elusive criminals to anticipate where they will strike next. Sometimes it works and sometimes it doesn't, but it's better than nothing in the absence of hard evidence.

This same technique is readily applied to the process of finding Easter eggs. Look for patterns. Figure out what the programmer is thinking:

◆ Has there been a big public event at the company?

◆ Is there a heated rivalry between this product and another product?

◆ Where were the Easter eggs in previous versions of the software?

◆ Has there been a big event in the news recently?

◆ Are there any political movements that effect this particular program or the company?

These could all be clues to hidden Easter eggs.

The Windows NT 3D Text Easter eggs are ideal examples. The key phrases in version 3.51 were "rock," "music," "beer" and "I love NT." In version 4.0 it was "volcano." Let's think a minute. Where is Microsoft located? It's in Redmond, a suburb of Seattle, Washington. To the pop-musical world, Seattle has come to be known as the "Grunge" capital. It also has a long tradition of rock and roll. Jimi Hendrix is buried there. Pearl Jam, Alice in Chains, Nirvana, and Soundgarden all came out of Seattle. Isn't it natural for "music" and "rock" to be potential triggers for secret features, since the programmers are probably into the Seattle music scene?

Also, the northwest is famous for its microbreweries, so it makes sense to hide a list of different beers as an Easter egg. The northwest is also renowned for it's mountains and outdoor sports. Skiing, snowboarding, mountain biking, hiking, and rock climbing are all popular sports in the area. So doesn't it make sense to hide a list of mountains as an Easter egg?

Plus, since there were Easter eggs in the 3D text screen saver in version 3.51, why wouldn't there be eggs in the same place for version 4.0? It's all a matter of figuring out patterns and what the programmers might be thinking. I wouldn't be surprised to find future Easter eggs about other things common to Seattle or the northwest. How about a list of coffees? Starbucks Coffee was founded in Seattle, and I'm sure the hard working Microsoft staff drinks plenty of it on their long shifts.

If you look for patterns and imagine yourself in the programmer's shoes, you could find some great Easter eggs.

How to think like a programmer

◆ Imagine yourself as the programmer of a certain piece of software. Maybe even set the mood a little. Make a huge pot of strong coffee and keep it within arms length. Stare at a screen and type frantically for several hours. Maybe even put up some cardboard around your desk to simulate an office cubicle. Whatever helps you become more in tune with your "inner programmer."

◆ Ask yourself, "Where am I programming?" A programmer in Phoenix, Arizona will have a drastically different living environment than someone in Fargo, North Dakota. A programmer for Netscape in Mountainview, California won't have the same surroundings as a Microsoft programmer in Redmond, Washington.

◆ Next ask, "What is special about my area?" The Windows NT 4.0 Easter egg demonstrates activities popular to the American northwest. A programmer in Texas might include things special about Texas, like barbecues, chili, oil, or cowboys. Likewise, a programmer in New York City might put something in about the Statue of Liberty, Times Square or hellish traffic. Every geographical area has its own special traits from which the programmer might draw for inspiration.

♦ Ask, "Who is my boss?" Programmers often like to poke a little fun at their managers and executives. Many a CEO has been the butt of a little humor from his employees. Figure out who the big boss is at the company that wrote software. This could be a potential clue to an Easter egg, especially if the CEO has been in the news a lot lately.

♦ Ask, "Who am I competing against?" Or for the realism of a programmer after a 14-hour day, "Who has the audacity to stand between me and complete world domination?!?" Many products have definite rivals. Netscape Navigator vs. Internet Explorer. Lotus 123 vs. Excel. WordPerfect vs. Word. Windows vs. Macintosh vs. UNIX. Intel vs. Motorola. The list goes on and on in the PC industry, and a rival product can easily be the butt of an Easter egg.

♦ Ask, "Has a big public event happened in my company recently?" Maybe two large companies merged, or one was bought out by the other. Programmers from one company might bear a grudge or they might want to commemorate the merger. A good subtle place to show their feelings about this event might be in an Easter egg.

♦ Ask, "Are there any controversial laws or propositions pending that would affect me?" The recently proposed Communications Decency Act created a storm of criticism and outrage within the software and Internet community.

It wouldn't surprise me a bit to find Easter eggs relating to it in various products, especially from small independent software companies. Another good example would be the proposition in California to decriminalize medicinal marijuana. Some smaller California-based software companies might use that in their Easter eggs.

◆ Ask, "What do I do for fun?" Granted, everybody is different and has fun in different ways. But there are some definite trends within the population of programmers.

Programmers are generally more aware and/or in love with technology. Most of them like nice stereo systems, home theaters, and cellular phones. They also tend to like science fiction more than most others, so don't be surprised to find a lot of Star Trek and Red Dwarf fans among them.

Any recreational activity a "techie" might enjoy is a good target for an Easter egg. Don't rule out outdoor, noncompetitive sports and activities as likely subjects. I've found a lot of programmers who like to hike, rock climb, mountain bike, and otherwise stay fit and active.

However, not many of them are fans of the big competitive sports, like football, baseball or basketball. I'm not trying to pigeonhole programmers into any one group, since everyone is indeed unique, but these are a few general trends I've noticed. However, any fun thing the programmer does in his spare time could be the basis for an Easter egg.

◆ Ask, "Who do I care about?" There have been eggs with dedications to the programmer's wife, mother or family. Any loved one might be included somehow in an Easter egg.

With these questions and a couple hours of meditation, you might achieve Zen with the programmer and be naturally drawn to the location of the Easter egg. Even if you aren't, at least you might have some clues to give your search new direction.

Snoop Around The Files

Since Easter eggs add hidden features to a program, it isn't at all surprising that they might add extra files to the program as well. How can you find these files? Easily, if you have some computer experience. Programs usually have all their files installed to the same folder or directory on a hard drive, so start by snooping around the files in that folder. Do you see any files with filenames that look out of place? For instance, is there a file called OJTRIAL.GIF in your spreadsheet's folder? This looks like a picture file that has something to do with the recent O.J. Simpson trial. Does that

NOTE

Here we start getting into techniques that require some computer skills. Before attempting this method, you should know how to browse around the files in your hard drive and open text files with a text editor, such as Notepad or Word.

sound like a common spreadsheet feature? Probably not, so open it up with a picture viewer and see what it is. It might be an Easter egg they threw in with the program files.

Looking at files themselves can yield humorous findings. A former professor of mine, Richard Pattis, was working on a robot simulator for a book he wrote in 1981. While writing the program, he got hooked on a singing group called "The Roches." So as a little personal whim, he decided to use that in his program. Whenever the user created a "world" for the robot to explore and saved the world to a file, the first thing in the file would be the word "ROCHES." Then in order to check which files were "world" files, the program would look for "ROCHES" as the first thing in the file.

Take a closer look at those files you just installed. You might find an egg hiding there.

Guide to exploring files

◆ Any file names that end in .GIF, .JPG, .JPEG, .TIFF or .BMP are picture files. They contain images in one format or another, and a good image viewer program should be able to display it for you.

I recommend LView, since it is available on the net as shareware that you can download for free, and it handles just about all picture formats known to man. If you see any of these with curious or suspicious looking names, go ahead and look at them. Heck, if you want, look at any of these files you come across. They might be Easter egg evidence.

◆ Any file name ending in .EXE, .COM or .BAT is a file you can run. If you find a file called "FIREWORKS.EXE" along with your accounting software, it might be an indication of an Easter egg. You can run the program by double-clicking on the file from Windows Explorer, but be warned that it might do anything, including something unwanted. Just be careful before running unknown code.

◆ Any files ending in .TXT are text files that you can open with a text editor, such as Windows's Notepad. Most text files are just documentation or help files, but they might contain Easter eggs or clues to their existence.

◆ Files ending in .CFG are probably configuration files. These are treated separately in the next section.

◆ Files ending in .HTM or .HTML are files used by Web browsers. Fire up your favorite web browser, such as Netscape, and open up the file to see what it looks like.

◆ Any .DOC files could either be Word documents or text files. Open them up with a good word processor to reveal their contents.

◆ A file ending in .RTF is a Rich Text Format file. This is a Microsoft document format, so open it with a good word processor.

Configuration Files

M ost programs have some sort of configuration or initialization file that the program uses to customize itself to your particular system. Games, for instance, usually want to know what kind of sound card is installed in your machine. This startup information is usually stored in a small configuration file. For Windows programs, these files can end in the extension INI. For 32-bit Windows 95 or Windows NT programs, the information will be stored somewhere in the system registry.

Sometimes you can get interesting and secret behavior by changing these settings. Now I know, according to the rules laid down at the start of this book, that changing the program files is not allowed.

This is still true. Changing the configuration files comes dangerously close to violating the rule, but the fact is, configuration files were meant to be, well,

WARNING

Before changing any configurations, it's a good idea to back up the file, so you can restore the original settings. While mucking around with configurations usually won't be harmful, always make sure you read the documentation first and aren't doing something decidedly destructive. There are no guarantees what will happen when a program sees something it doesn't recognize.

configured! Changing these settings might not be comfortable for some people, but it's a perfectly valid way of invoking Easter eggs.

How to view and modify files ending in .CFG or .CNF

◆ These files don't usually follow a standard format shared by all software manufacturers. You might find these files with DOS-based software or some Windows software. Open it up with a text editor to view and modify the file. Usually, a .CFG or .CNF file will be organized into groups of "<key> = <value>" pairs, where <key> is some parameter used by the program and <value> is the value the key is given. Try experimenting with key words and phrases as values for some keys.

How to view and modify files ending in .INI

◆ .INI files are usually used by software written for Windows 3.1 and below, but some software for Windows 95 and NT might still use these. .INI files have a definite format and structure. Open one up with a text editor and you will see a structure like this:

```
[<Heading_1>]
<key_1> = <value_1>
<key_2> = <value_2>
<key_3> = <value_3>
...

[<Heading_2>]

...
```

◆ Headings are enclosed in brackets, each followed by a series of <key> = <value> pairs. Let's take a look at a fragment from a genuine .INI file. This one is from a file called "userdef.ini" used by Netscape:

```
[Settings]
Beeps=Yes
;;; timeout in secs of invitation dialog
InvitationTimeout=20
PhotoDefault=userdflt.bmp
PhotoDial=userwait.bmp
DLSDefaultServer=dls.netscape.com
DLSServerWebPage=http://home.netscape.com/
   comprod/products/communicator/conference/phonebook
[DLL Plugins]
Chat=nschat32.dll
File Exchange=nsfilx32.dll
Collaborative Surfing=nssurf32.dll
Whiteboard=nswb32.dll
Speakerphone=nsfone32.dll
```

♦ As you can see, there are two headings here, *Settings* and *DLL Plugins*. Under each heading are keys and their associated values. Note: On the third line, you will notice three semicolons (;;;) followed by a comment. In an .INI file, anything on a line following a semicolon (;) is considered a comment and has no effect on the program.

♦ Just from a quick scan of this, you may notice some things that would be easy for you to try changing. *PhotoDefault* is set to *userdflt.bmp*. .BMP files are picture files, so try searching around in the directory for this picture file. Maybe you'll notice other picture files in the same directory. If so, you could try changing *userdflt.bmp* to another picture file.

♦ Maybe you won't find an Easter egg by changing these .INI files, or maybe you don't feel comfortable changing these critical files around without documentation. That's fine. At the very least, an .INI file can give you a lot of clues and information about how a program works. It can point you to files used by the program and clue you in on how they are used. A clever egg hunter can use this knowledge to take his search in new directions.

How to view and modify the System Registry

In Windows 95 and Windows NT, programs can store their configuration information in a large, organized database known as the System Registry. A Registry editor ships with both Win 95 and NT that allows you to view and modify the data in this Registry. Here is how to start up the Registry editor:

◆ Go to the Start Menu and select **Run...** If you are running Windows NT 3.51 or before, go to the **File** menu of the Program Manager and select **Run...**

◆ If you are running Windows 95, type "regedit" in the box and click OK. If you are running Windows NT, type "regedt32" and click OK.

This will start up the Registry Editor. It will look similar to Windows Explorer, with a tree structure on the left and data values on the right. Figure 1 shows what the Registry Editor looks like when I start it up on my Windows 95 PC.

Figure 1
The Registry Editor

111

Now I'm sure this all looks very cryptic and hard to understand. You're right, it is. That's why Microsoft and other software vendors specifically tell their customers not to modify the Registry settings. So for now we'll only be looking through the Registry for clues to Easter eggs without changing anything—your computer will be safe.

◆ There are two branches of the Registry that will be most interesting in your hunt for configuration information. First is HKEY_LOCAL_MACHINE, which contains configuration information for the entire machine, and HKEY_CURRENT_USER, which contains configuration information specific to you, the current user. If you expand each of these branches of the tree by clicking on the little plus sign next to them, you will see a folder called "Software" in each. Expand the "Software" folder and you will see a bunch of folders with the names of your software programs. Search through the folder of your software product to find its configuration information. The next figure shows what my screen looks like when I looked for Netscape Navigator under HKEY_CURRENT_USER.

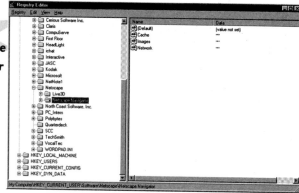

Figure 2
Finding Netscape
Navigator under
*HKEY_*
CURRENT
_USER

How do we find and view the actual configuration information? Well, just keep expanding the branches of the tree until you can't do so anymore. When you select these final folders, the right portion of the window will display the configuration information in that folder in the familiar <key> <value> style. The next figure shows what happens when I look at my user settings for Netscape Navigator.

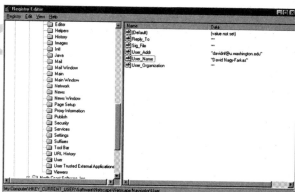

Figure 3
User Settings for
Netscape
Navigator

◆ As you can see, my E-mail address is in there, as well as my name. When I set up Navigator, I didn't enter an organization or a signature file (for email). What might happen if I changed my user name to "Mark Andreesen" and my organization to "Netscape?" Well, probably nothing, but Mark is the president and founder of Netscape, so you never know. Remember though, CHANGING REGISTRY CAN BE DANGEROUS AND MAY INVALIDATE YOUR WARRANTEE OR TECH SUPPORT PRIVILEGES. Only start changing things if you are very adventurous, and ALWAYS write down what the original registry values are before changing them.

◆ You say you're a brave, daring soul who wants to start changing settings in the Registry? You're not afraid of the Software Police? Tech. support is for wussies? Okay then, here's how you can modify the Registry properly.

◆ To open any value for modification, highlight the key and choose **Modify** from the **Edit** menu, or double click on the key. This will bring up a dialog box where you can edit the entry. Registry entries can be one of three types: strings, binary values or DWORDS, and this type will be on the title bar of the modification window.

My advice is to leave any binary values alone, because you really have NO idea how they is being used. DWORDS are just numbers, so you can type in a new number either in decimal (base 10, like everyday numbers we are used to) or hexadecimal (base 16, for experienced computer geeks only).

Strings are strings of text, and you can type a word or phrase of your choosing as the value. Usually with strings, you can guess what sort of text the program is looking for, such as a name, email address, or file name. Remember to write down the old value, in case you start the program up and all hell breaks loose. Restoring the Registry settings to their original values will usually fix things.

◆ For those who don't want to modify Registry settings with wild abandon (like me), feel free to use the Registry editor to just browse around. You may find some interesting clues to Easter eggs, or even just a better knowledge of how the program is working. What if you found a key in the Registry titled "Dancing Bear" and it's value was "Off." I know I would be curious to see what would happen if it was "On."

Command Line Parameters

In today's point-and-click world, command line parameters have become a thing of the past, except for die-hard computer aficionados. In the old days of DOS and UNIX, to start a program you would type its name. For example, to start WordPerfect, you would simply type "wp" and press enter.

However, you could start up programs with special options by adding command line parameters. Say you wanted to start WordPerfect and open a file called "mypaper.doc." As a shortcut you might be able to type "wp -o mypaper.doc." This would tell WordPerfect to start up *and* open the file at the same time.

Command line parameters performed a similar function to the hot keys we use today. They were shortcuts for common operations or extra features. So why not add Easter eggs for hidden command line parameters? If you have any old software lying around, try starting it up with some wacky command line parameters. For example, when installing the game Wing Commander 3, you can test your sound card. The sound test is a loud voice shouting "Mitchell!" If you start the game with "Mitchell" as a command line parameter (instead of typing "wc3" to start the game, you type "wc3 -mitchell") you have access to all sorts of secret abilities during the game.

Give it a try with that old DOS program you haven't used in years. It just may surprise you.

How to invoke programs using command line parameters

◆ If you are using Windows 3.1 or 95, start up an MS-DOS Prompt. If you are using Windows NT, start up a Command Prompt.

◆ Many people aren't used to a command line interface, since they've gotten into computers after Windows and Macintosh were mainstream. At a command line prompt, you have to do everything by typing in commands. Here is a brief summary of some key commands you will need:

Key command	Function/Purpose
dir	Lists the files and directories within the current directory. "Dir /p" will list them page by page, if the list is so long it scrolls of your screen. "Dir /ad" will list only directories.
cd **chdir**	Changes the current directory to the one you specify. For example, if you start at the beginning of your C drive and type "cd windows" you will be moved into the windows directory of your system. "Cd.." will take you back one directory level and "cd \" will take you all the way back to the start of your directory structure.

◆ There are many more commands that do just about everything you could desire. Check your documentation if you are interested in further investigation, but the above should be enough to get you started.

◆ Go into the directory of your program by using the "cd" command.

◆ Use "dir" to get a listing of all the files in the current directory. Note any files ending in .EXE, .COM or .BAT. For most modern programs, the file that you run will end in .EXE.

◆ Type the program filename at the command prompt. For example, once you find NETSCAPE.EXE, then you can type "netscape" at the prompt to start it up.

♦ Try running the program with command line parameters you make up. For example, if you type "netscape www.abacuspub.com" Netscape will start up and jump right to Abacus's home page. Many programs have different options you can invoke with several different parameters. The "dir" command described earlier has many different command line parameters. Type "dir /?" for a list of them. Try starting your program with "?", "-?" or "/?" as command line parameters. Some programs use this to give you a list of the command line parameters they support.

♦ You can also combine command line parameters together. For example, typing "dir /p /w /ad" will list only directories in the current directory in wide screen format, page by page.

♦ Some command line parameters require values, so try using some values you make up. For example, suppose a program called "wordmaster" takes a parameter in the format "/t=<title>" where <title> is the title of your document. Maybe a special value for <title> will invoke an Easter egg.

The command line technique is most useful in older DOS-based programs, but I've seen some interesting behavior from Windows programs too. Sometimes Windows programs have a lot of command line options so that an automatic testing program can test them easier. As a tester, it's a lot easier to write a simple script that will automatically start up a program with different command line parameters than it is to sit there and click all over the screen repeatedly. Therefore, who knows what little command line parameters may be lying dormant in your favorite software package.

Using A Resource Editor

Using a Resource Editor is one of the most powerful tools to finding Easter eggs in modern Windows software. However, it requires special software and intimate knowledge of how Windows programs work. If you aren't a very experienced computer user, just skip on to the next section since you really shouldn't be trying this without more experience. If you are an experienced user or a developer, read on! This is the most efficient way of finding Easter eggs in an unexplored piece of software.

In the Windows programming world, a program file has "resources" embedded inside it. These could be bitmap pictures, menus, dialog boxes, etc. With the right programmer's tools, you can peek at the raw resources within a program file. I'm a Visual C++ user, so my example will be for those of you using Visual C++ 4.0. However, any other good development environment, like Borland C++, ought to come with similar capabilities.

Using Visual C++ to view and edit program resources

◆ Start up Visual C++. Select "Open" from the **File** menu.

◆ In the "Files of Type" box, select "Executable Files (*.exe, *.dll, *.ocx)."

◆ Browse around your hard drive for your program's files, including any .DLL files it might be using.

◆ When you've found a target file, open it by double-clicking it or highlighting it and selecting OK.

◆ Visual C++ will show you a tree of resources. This can include bitmaps, icons, dialog boxes, menus, and other sorts of resources used by the program. In the picture below, I opened a random file called "disptest.exe" located in the msdev\bin directory. You should have the same file installed, so go ahead and open it up and take a look around.

Figure 4
The
"disptest.exe"
file in the
msdev\bin
directory

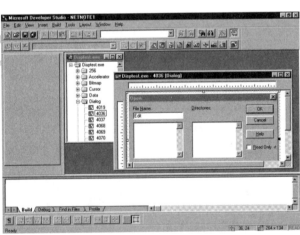

◆ Look through the Dialog folder. Visual C++ lets you view all of the dialog boxes used in the program. If you find one that looks suspicious, it could have something to do with an Easter egg.

◆ Look through the Accelerator folder. This contains all of the hot keys accepted by the program. If you compare this list of hot keys to the list of documented hot keys and find some extra ones, then you may have struck gold! Try out these extra hot keys with the program and see what happens.

◆ Look through the Icons and Bitmaps. You can find many clues to the existence of an Easter egg simply by finding a funny or out of place picture as an icon or bitmap in the program.

◆ Look through the Cursors. Again, look for unusual or suspicious cursor types that you've never encountered before. Maybe some action will turn your cursor into a picture of Bill Gates, if Bill Gates appears as one of the cursors.

◆ Examine the String Table. It contains a huge table of words and phrases used within the program. Scan it for incriminating Easter egg evidence.

◆ Browse the Menu folder. Maybe you'll find a menu or some menu items you've never found before, which could have something to do with an Easter egg.

By looking through a program's resources, you can get an amazing amount of information about the program's inner workings without even running it! If you've got the right tools, a resource editor can work wonders in your egg hunt.

Side Note: The resource editor will also allow you to CHANGE all of these values. You could really screw things up by deleting or modifying a crucial resource, so just be sure not to change anything. Or if you're a brave hacker type, you can try modifying resources. Remember, **modifying resources is not a valid step in a true Easter egg**. The original program can't be modified in a genuine egg. But I've been known to hack around a little and playfully change a program's icons here and there for my own amusement. It can be a recreational hacker's paradise, IF you know what you're doing.

Hex Editor

Don't worry, there's no occult magic here. This is the tried and true method for die-hard hackers everywhere in the world. A hex editor is a program that lets you view and change individual bits and bytes within a file. A hacker needs a good hex editor just like a secretary needs a good word processor. It lets an experienced user see exactly what the machine sees.

Granted, when most of us look at this code, it looks messier than a teenager's bedroom. But the trained eye can actually understand what is going on and find hidden secrets this way. It's not easy; I wouldn't do it. But I mention it because it is possible and Easter eggs have been found this way. I can't give an example here because every program is entirely different when using this method. Besides, if you're good enough to find Easter eggs this way, then you're probably breaking into secret government files or some such instead of reading this book.

Let The Hunt Begin!

How do you feel? Are you excited? You now have a full set of tools to help you in the fun and habit-forming recreational pastime of Easter egg hunting! Several methods of finding Easter eggs have been outlined. The majority of Easter eggs can be discovered using these methods, but as computers change, so will the eggs. Frankly, some Easter eggs are too obscure to be discovered in any way except through blind luck. Use whatever methods you feel comfortable with, and don't be afraid to ask for help and advice from others. Go to it, my friends, and hunt down these elusive gems of the software world. It's just like Easter Sunday when you were a kid, isn't it?

Part II

Existing Easter Eggs

Introduction To Part II

One of the great things about Easter eggs is that you don't always have to find them yourself! Thousands of other Easter egg hunters help you track them down every day. Thanks to the great communication medium of the Internet, we Easter egg lovers can easily share our knowledge. If you don't feel like searching for eggs yourself, don't worry! Plenty of us out here are far more obsessed than you may be, and you can benefit from our efforts.

This section is an indexed list of all the PC Easter eggs I know about, which are also online at the Easter Egg Archive : http://weber.u.washington.edu/~davidnf/eggs. From Adobe to Zork, if there is an egg I know about, it's in here. Check this list before you start hunting on your own; it will save you a lot of time and effort. In fact, check the online version often for new Easter eggs in the latest and greatest products if you can't find them here. Many game cheat codes, not mentioned here, can also be found in the Easter Egg Archive.

... visit The Easter Egg Archive on the World Wide Web... *http://weber.u. washington.edu/ ~davidnf/eggs/*

Enjoy these eggs! Read the following pages and activate any eggs that may be on your computer. In fact, you'll probably find many that you can demonstrate to friends on their computers. Spread the wealth of knowledge and enable these great programming tidbits to be enjoyed by all! Happy hunting!

Contents Of Part II

134

Games Easter Eggs 205

138

Windows 3.1 Easter Eggs

> ## Windows 3.1
> (Microsoft Corporation)
> **Who Wrote This Program?**
> **From David Nagy-Farkas**

1. Press [Ctrl] + [Alt] + [Shift]. Don't let up on any of these keys throughout this process.

2. Go to the **Help** menu of the Program Manager and select **About Program Manager**.

3. There should be a nice colorful Microsoft Windows logo in the upper-left corner of the window. Double-click on one of the four colors in the logo and click [OK].

4. Repeat steps two and three, clicking on a different color in the logo. The bottom of the window should change to display an animated Windows flag and different text.

5. Repeat steps two and three again, clicking on still another color in the logo. The bottom of the window will change once more to display a person presenting the programmers' names on a chalkboard.

6. Repeat this whole procedure using different color combinations. You should see different people in the final screen, and even a bear (the unofficial mascot of Microsoft programmers) if you're lucky.

Minesweeper (Windows 3.1)
(Microsoft Corporation)
Amaze your Friends by "Sensing" Mines
Submitted by Troy McLucas

1. Run Minesweeper and type "xyzzy."

2. Press the left Shift key.

3. Look at the most upper-left pixel. Since this pixel resides on the background wallpaper, you may have to minimize or shrink Program Manager to see it. When the cursor is on a square containing a mine, the pixel will turn off. When the pixel is on, there is no mine in the square under the cursor.

4. This is known to work under Windows 3.1 and Windows for Workgroups 3.11, but Minesweeper under Windows 95 was changed and this trick won't work under that interface.

Solitaire (Windows 3.1)
(Microsoft Corporation)
Cheater!
Submitted by Chon Dolan

1. Open Solitaire

2. Play with settings Vegas, Keep Score, Draw 3, Not Timed.

3. Hold down [Ctrl] + [Alt] + [Shift].

4. Click on the deck of cards. Instead of drawing three cards, you get one card at a time, yet can still go through the deck three times.

5. Win, win, win!

Windows 95
Easter Eggs

Windows 95 Easter Eggs

> **Windows 95**
> (Microsoft Corporation)
> **Team Credits**
> **Submitted by Eli Smith**

1. Right-click on the desktop.

2. Select **New \ Folder**.

3. Title the folder "and now, the moment you've all been waiting for."

4. Right-click on this folder and select **Rename** from the pop-up menu.

5. Rename it "we proudly present for your viewing pleasure."

6. Rename it again as "The Microsoft Windows 95 Product Development Team!"

7. Be sure to type it as it is here, and turn on your speakers, if you have them.

8. Open the folder to display the credits of Windows 95. This folder will remain available so you can view the credits anytime by opening the folder.

Windows 95
(Microsoft Corporation)
Taskbar Animation
Submitted by Matt

1. Exit all programs.

2. Press [Ctrl] + [Alt] + [Del].

3. Select **Explorer**.

4. Select **End Task**.

5. When asked to shut down, choose No.

6. Repeat steps two through five until an Explorer error message appears.

7. Choose **End Task** in the error dialogue box.

8. Watch the animation in the taskbar.

Minesweeper (Windows 95)
(Microsoft Corporation)
Stop the Clock
Submitted by Sir Twist

1. Run Minesweeper.

2. Click on a square to start the timer.

3. Hold down both mouse buttons and press [Esc].

4. Solve Minesweeper in the best recorded time!

Windows 95
(Microsoft Corporation)
Where's the START button?
Submitted by Judge Insane

1. Click the START button.

2. Press Esc.

3. Press Alt + -.

4. Select **Close**.

5. To get the START button back, restart Windows.

Windows 95
(Microsoft Corporation)
Move the Start Button
Submitted by Hillel Aftel

1. Click on the "Start" button.

2. Press Esc.

3. Press Alt + - + , + .

4. In the menu that pops up, select "Move."

5. Now you can use the mouse or the arrow keys to move the start button just like you would normally move a window!

Windows 95
(Microsoft Corporation)
Change to Mac-like Folder Icons
Submitted by X

1. Choose a folder with many folders inside.

2. Choose "Select All."

3. Press Alt + Del + Shift.

4. Press Y for the message.

Windows NT
Easter Eggs

Windows NT v. 3.51
(Microsoft Corporation)
J'Aime NT, Me Gusta NT. . .
From David Nagy-Farkas

1. Select **Control Panel** from the Main Menu.

2. Select **Desktop**.

3. Select **Open GL 3D Text** as your screen saver type.

4. Click **Options** to configure the screen saver's settings.

5. Change the text that the screen saver will display to "I love NT."

6. Either wait for the screen saver to activate or hit "test." The names of all the programmers will float in and out in 3D text.

7. This also works in many foreign languages, such as "j'aime NT." If "I love NT" doesn't work, try "I like NT." For instance, "Me amo NT" doesn't work, but "Me gusta NT" does.

Windows NT v.3.51

(Microsoft Corporation)

More 3D Text Eggs

Submitted by Bo Stephens and Barrie Smith

1. Select **Control Panel \ Desktop**.

2. Select the 3d Test (Open GL) screen saver.

3. Click on **Options** to configure the settings.

4. Change the text to "Beer" and activate the screen saver.

5. Change the text to "Rock" and activate the screen saver.

6. Change the text to "Music" and activate the screen saver.

Windows NT v. 4.0

(Microsoft Corporation)

Volcano

From David Nagy-Farkas

1. Select the "3D Text (OpenGL)" screen saver.

2. Click on "Settings."

3. Enter "volcano" in the text field.

4. Click OK.

5. Click "Preview" or wait for screen saver to activate.

Windows NT v.3.5
(Microsoft Corporation)
Teapot
Submitted by Alan Grainger

1. Select **Control Panel \ Desktop**.

2. Select **3D Pipes (Open GL)** as the screen saver.

3. Click **Setup** and set the joint style to mixed.

4. When the screen saver activates, look closely. Every once in a while a "teapot joint" will appear.

MS-DOS
Easter Eggs

Microsoft Disk Operating System prior to 6.2
(Microsoft Corporation)
Who Helps the Helper?
Submitted by Alan Hamilton

1. Run MSD.EXE. If you have Windows 3.1, use the program in the x:\windows directory, not x:\dos.

2. Select **Help/About**.

3. Press F1.

4. This joke has been removed from Versions 6.2 and later.

Application
Easter Eggs

Access 2.0
(Microsoft Corporation)
Puzzles
Submitted by Patti Johnson

1. Create a new database titled "db1.mdb."

2. Create four tables named "a," "cc," "e" and "ss" (they can have anything in them).

3. Open this database.

4. Select **Help \ About**.

5. Hold down [Ctrl] + [Shift] and double-right-click on the key picture.

Access for Windows 95
(Microsoft Corporation)
Magic Eight Ball
Submitted by John Hansen

1. Open any database in Microsoft Access.

2. Select the Macros tab and click "New."

3. In the macro editing window, make a change and save the macro as "Magic Eight Ball."

4. Select View/Toolbars... and choose "Customize..."

Continued on next page

5. Scroll all the way to the bottom of the list of toolbar options to "All Macros." In the opposite window, click and drag your macro to the toolbar above.

6. Before closing the window, right-click your new macro button and select "Choose button image." Select the Eight Ball icon.

7. Close all windows except the database window.

8. Ask your computer a yes-or-no question.

9. Click the button to see the answer!

Access

(Microsoft Corporation)

Make my Computer Smile

Submitted by Scott Seltzer

---

1. In **Help**, go to **Find**.

2. Search for the word "happiness" or "Smile."

3. Although it isn't in the Help index, "Make my computer smile" comes up.

America On-line v. 3.0
(America Online, Incorporated)
Hidden Version Information
Submitted by John Seg

1. Open the About box from the Help menu.

2. Hold the Ctrl key and press R. This is the revision number.

3. Do the same, but instead of R type T. This will give you all of the TODs on your system and their revision #s. Use this to see if you have things like the browser or other AOL tools.

Amipro 3.0 and 3.1
(Lotus Development Group)
Elvis Chases Donut
Submitted by Josh Simar

1. In Amipro, go to Tools/User Setup.

2. In the initials box type "GPB" (upper case only).

3. Now go to Help/About AmiPro.

4. Hold Ctrl + Shift and press the Function key corresponding to the day of the week (F1=Sunday).

5. While still holding Ctrl + Shift, type "SHANK."

6. Have fun!

Automap
(Microsoft Corporation)
Spin Out
Submitted by Mars

1. Run Automap.

2. Hold [Shift] while selecting **Help \ About**.

3. On the right side of the dialog box, a spinning red car will appear.

Automap
(Microsoft Corporation)
Secret Settings
Submitted by Robin

1. Run Automap Streets

2. Click on **Help**.

3. Hold [Shift] and click **System Info**.

4. A secret technical settings window appears.

BeyondMail 2.x
(Banyan Systems, Incorporated)
Developer Credits
Submitted by Rob McCauley

1. Run the following command within Windows:

2. \Bmail\program\bmailw.exe -e kitchensink

Borland C++ 4.0 and up
(Borland International, Incorporated)
Credits and Dedication
Submitted by Alan Hamilton

1. In Borland C++, open **Help \ About...**

2. Press Alt + I.

3. In 4.0 a credits screen appears; in 4.5x it's a dedication screen.

Borland C++ 4.5 and above
(Borland International, Incorporated)
A Tribute
Anonymous submission

1. In Borland C++, select **Help \ About**.

2. Hold down Ctrl + Shift.

3. Double-click the icon in the upper-left corner.

Central Point Desktop
(Central Point Software)
Fireworks!
Submitted by Justin DeVore

1. Select **About Desktop** from the program's **Help** menu.

2. Hold Ctrl + Shift and simultaneously click both mouse buttons on the desktop icon.

3. A fireworks show begins, listing the developers.

4. Click the left mouse button where you want the fireworks to appear!

5. Click the right mouse button to change the fireworks scheme!

Impromptu
Cognos, Incorporated
Hidden Credits
Submitted by Jim Kadingo

1. Launch Impromptu.

2. Select **Help \ About Impromptu**.

3. Right-click on the logo.

Compton's Interactive Encyclopedia
(SoftKey International, Incorporated)
Credits Slideshow
Anonymous submission

1. Go to the top of any List Box; Contents is a good one with which to try this.

2. Select the third item with a single mouse click.

3. Type three capital "Z"s.

Connectix QuickCam
(Connectix Corporation)
Credits
Submitted by Alan Ashton

1. Launch QuickMovie or QuickPict (version 2.1 or later).

2. Select **Help/About**.

3. Press (Shift) + (Ctrl) + (J) to open a large dialog box containing the credits.

Corel Draw 5.0
(Corel Corporation)
He is alive!
Submitted by Ed Luczyki

1. Start Corel Draw.

2. Select **About** from the **Help** menu.

3. Double-click one of the icons.

4. You will see the Corel balloon and a hand with a lever.

5. Click the right mouse button and hold.

6. The balloon will rise with a banner.

7. Right-click the mouse and enjoy.

8. Try it on different days and at different times of the day.

PhotoPaint 5.0
(Corel Corporation)
Flying Balloon
Submitted by Robert Prom

1. Select **About Corel Photo-Paint** from the **Help** menu.

2. Hold [Ctrl] + [Shift] and double-click the Corel balloon.

3. A blue screen will appear with a parachuting Elvis.

4. Hold down the right mouse button to light the balloon.

5. Double-click the dark sky icon (across the balloon in the upper-right corner) to fly the balloon in a dark sky.

6. Press [Esc] to exit this egg.

PhotoPaint 6.0
(Corel Corporation)
Design Team Blimp
Submitted by Mark Hagenbrok

1. Click **About** in PhotoPaint's **Help** menu.

2. Hold [Ctrl] + [Alt] for a blimp flashing the design credits.

3. Hold [Ctrl] + [Shift] for a balloon and parachuting Elvis.

4. Hold [Shift] + [Alt] for a balloon and fireworks.

Dbase 5
(Borland International, Incorporated)
Anti-Fox Pro
Submitted by Bernard Timbal

1. Go to the **About** menu.

2. Enter "Alt fox."

3. The OK button will transform itself into a guillotine and decapitate the animated fox.

Delphi
(Borland International, Incorporated)
Hidden Information
Submitted by Martin Bouchard

1. Make the About box appear by selecting **Help \ About**.

2. Hold the Alt key and type "version" to see the version number.

3. Holding Alt, type "and" for a picture of Anders Hejlsberg.

4. Holding Alt, type "team" for a list of those behind Delphi.

5. Holding Alt, type "developers" for a list of the R&D folks specifically.

Encarta 96 World Atlas
(Microsoft Corporation)
Pictures of People
Submitted by Duncan Lawler

1. From the **Find** menu, select **Place**.

2. Type "Necropolis of Mir" in the Go to dialog box.

3. Press `Enter`.

4. Use the zoom tool to go to 509km (you'll have to type it in).

5. In the credits screen, click on one of the pictures to see the people in that group.

Energizer Bunny Screen Saver
Eveready Battery Company
Valentine Egg
Submitted by Peter Morrison

1. Wait until February 14th or change the date on your computer.

2. Turn on the screen saver and hearts will float away from the bunny.

Application Easter Eggs

Eudora Light 3.0 (32-bit version, maybe 16-bit also)
Qualcomm, Incorporated
Funky Credits
Submitted by Matthew DeMizio

1. Open **Help/About...**

2. Click on the button marked "More Credits."

3. Press ⌃Ctrl to make them funky.

4. Press ⇧Shift to speed them up.

Eudora Pro
(Qualcomm, Incorporated)
Cool Credits
Submitted by E. Scott FitzGerald

1. Launch Eudora and go to **Help/About**.

2. Click the "More Credits" button.

3. When the scrolling starts, press ⌃Ctrl to see the names change.

174

Excel 4.0
(Microsoft Corporation)
Kill the Competitor's Bugs
Submitted by Douglas Ghormley

1. Call up a blank worksheet with a standard tool bar.

2. Click the right mouse button.

3. From the **Customize** option, select **Custom** and drag the solitaire icon to an empty spot on the tool bar.

4. Under **Assign to Tool**, click [OK], click **Close**, then hold [Ctrl] + [Alt] + [Shift] while clicking the solitaire icon.

Excel 95
(Microsoft Corporation)
Hall of Tortured Souls
Submitted by John Gaskell

1. Open Excel 95 with a blank worksheet.

2. Go down to the 95th row and select the entire row.

3. Tab over to column B.

4. Select **Help \ About**.

5. Hold [Ctrl] + [Alt] + [Shift] and click on the tech support button.

6. Enter the Hall of Tortured Souls.

7. At the end of the hall with the programmers' names, turn 180 degrees, type "excelkfa" and walk through the wall to see the pictures.

Excel 97
(Microsoft Corporation)
Flight to Credits
Anonymous Submission

1. Open a new worksheet and press F5.

2. Type "X97:L97" and press Enter.

3. Press the Tab key.

4. Hold Ctrl + Shift and click on the Chart Wizard button in the toolbar.

5. Use the mouse to fly—right button forward/left button reverse.

HomeSite 2.0
(Bradbury Software)
Little Easter Egg
Submitted by Nick Bradbury

1. Open HomeSite 2.0.

2. Select **Help/About**.

3. Press Ctrl + H.

4. Double-click on the HomeSite logo.

5. Have fun!

Hot Dog Pro v.3.0.9
(Sausage Software)
Brian
Submitted by Blaze Ignatowicz

1. Go to Help/About.

2. Double-click on the Hot Dog logo.

3. Double-click on Brian's picture.

Illustrator 6.0
(Adobe Systems, Inc.)
Colorful Display
Submitted by Robert Jolly

1. Select "About Adobe Illustrator" from the **Help** menu.

2. Double click on the Adobe logo in the top-left corner.

3. Enjoy!

Internet Phone v.3.x
(VocalTec, Incorporated)
Development Team
Submitted by Andrey Yanpolski

1. In Internet Phone open the **About** box from the **Help** menu.

2. Use the right mouse button to drag the icon on the right of the dialog box onto the left icon.

cc:Mail
(Lotus Development Corporation
Developer Credits
Submitted by Jim Kadingo

1. Login to cc:Mail

2. Select **Help**, then **About cc:Mail**.

3. Click anywhere in the about screen where the cursor appears as a question mark.

mIRC 4.0
Khaled Mardam-Bey
Follow the Bouncing Ball
Submitted by Jake Hawkins

1. Go to the **Help** pull-down menu.

2. Click **About**.

3. Right-click on **mIRC 4.0**.

---

mIRC

Khaled Mardam-Bey

Squeak

Submitted by Powdered Toast Man

---

1. Click on **Help** from the toolbar.

2. Select "About..."

3. Click on the end of Khaled's nose.

4. *Squeak!*

---

mIRC

Khaled Mardam-Bey

Stuffed Animal

Submitted by Jarod

---

1. Choose "About..." from the **Help** menu.

2. Press [Enter] five times.

3. Khaled's face turns into his faithful stuffed animal!

---

mIRC

Khaled Mardam-Bey

Cool Sayings

Submitted by Justin

---

1. Find the About icon.

2. Right-click this icon.

3. It's cool!

mIRC

Khaled Mardam-Bey

The Elusive Pet

Submitted by Matthew DeMizio

1. Select **About** from the **Help** menu.

2. Type "arnie."

mIRC

Khaled Mardam-Bey

Cool Message

Submitted by White Vampire

1. Put the cursor over the little yellow button on the taskbar.

2. Right click.

Organizer 1.0

(Lotus Development Corporation

Burn the Evidence

Submitted by Susan Ehrenfeld

1. Hold down $\boxed{\text{Shift}}$ + $\boxed{\text{Ctrl}}$ + $\boxed{\text{Alt}}$.

2. Triple-click on the trash can in the lower-left-hand corner.

3. After the flames die, you should see the developer credits.

4. Press $\boxed{\text{Esc}}$ to escape.

Organizer 2.x
(Lotus Development Corporation
Flame
Submitted by Ian Armstrong

1. Type the text "Flame" into any wordprocessor (e.g., Notepad).

2. Highlight the text and copy it to the clipboard (Ctrl + C).

3. In Organizer, you will see that the clipboard icon (left of screen) has a picture on it.

4. Drag this picture icon to the trashcan.

5. A list of developers will replace the main Organizer book.

Notes 4.0 (32-bit)
(Lotus Development Corporation)
Payroll
Submitted by Jay Rowland

1. Click **Help**, then choose **About Notes**.

2. When the dialog box opens type "Release the power."

3. This may also work on some 16-bit systems.

Notes 4.0 Workstation
(Lotus Development Corporation
Elvis Fan
Submitted by Ken Cunliffe

1. Click **Help**.

2. Click **About Notes**.

3. Type "elvis is not dead" in lower-case letters.

4. Roy Ozzie's head appears and starts spewing credits.

Microsoft Exchange Server
(Microsoft Corporation)
Phoenix
Submitted by Doug Straus

1. Telnet to an Exchange server's SMTP port 25 (ex: telnet exchange.microsoft.com:25).

2. Type "phoenix" and press [Enter].

3. Repeat twice more.

Microsoft Office v.4.3
(Microsoft Corporation)
Hi, Mom!
Submitted by Susie Ehrenfeld

1. Click **About Microsoft Office**.

2. Hold down `Ctrl` + `Shift`.

3. Double-click the MS Office icon in the upper-left-hand corner.

4. The MS Office opening plate should appear.

5. Click anywhere on the plate.

6. The developers give their best to their mothers.

Office 95
(Microsoft Corporation)
The Four Best Mothers
Submitted by Gavin W. Boxall

1. Open the Office 95 toolbar.

2. Right-click on the logo in the top-left corner.

3. Click **About Microsoft Office**. This will show you the license screen and product ID information.

4. Hold `Ctrl` + `Shift` and double-click the Office 95 logo. The Office 95 title screen pops up.

5. Click on the title screen to close it.

6. The license screen has changed—Hi Mom!

Office (Toolbar)
(Microsoft Corporation)
Splash Screen
Submitted by Junben Bajuyo

1. Right-click on the small jigsaw puzzle at the upper left corner to the toolbar.

2. Click on "About Microsoft Office."

3. Press `Ctrl` + `Alt` + `Shift` then double-click on the MS Office Logo.

Systems Management Server
(Microsoft Corporation)
Hidden Something
Submitted by Tony Guerrero

1. Start the Microsoft SMS System Administrator.

2. Click on **Help** in the main menu bar.

3. Select **About SMS Administrator**.

4. When you see the spinning globe, type "Hermes" (don't click the `OK` button).

5. The credits for MS SMS Administrator will appear. If you wait until the end (and have completely filled out the registration information) you'll see your name listed as well.

> **Netscape Navigator**
> **Netscape Communications Corporation**
> **General Egg**
> **Submitted by Junben Bajuyo**

1. Load Netscape.

2. Open the URL "about:abcdef" ("abcdef" can be just about any text).

> **Netscape Navigator**
> **Netscape Communications Corporation**
> **The Netscape Folks**
> **Submitted by Adina Gordon**

1. Type "about:photo" into the location box for a photo of the Netscape folks.

2. Type "about:authors" into the location box for a list of the program's authors.

> **Netscape 1.1 and later**
> **Netscape Communications Corporation**
> **The Fishcam**
> **Submitted by Nick Van Dorsten**

1. Once your are in Netscape and online, just press Ctrl + Alt + F, and you'll go to the fishcam (fishlovers!—be sure to bookmark this page!).

Netscape Navigator

Netscape Communications Corporations

Variation on a Theme

Submitted by Ken

1. Type "about:mozilla" into the location field.

Netscape Navigator 3.0

Netscape Communications Corporation

More About: Eggs

Submitted by Tony Wooster

1. Load Navigator.

2. For the Netscape logo, type "about:logo" in the location field.

3. For the java logo, type "about:javalogo" in the location field.

4. For the Quicktime logo, type "about:qtlogo" in the location field.

5. For the RSA Encryption logo, type "about:rsalogo" in the location field.

Netscape Navigator

Netscape Communications Corporation

History List

Submitted by Aaron Breckenridge

1. Type "about:global" in the location field.

Netscape Navigator
Netscape Communications Corporation
International Mozilla
Submitted by Frederik De Bleser

1. In the location field, type "about:francaise to see Mozilla on a table drinking wine.

2. Type "about:deutsch" to see Mozilla in lederhosen.

3. This may work with other languages as well...

Netscape Navigator
Netscape Communications Corporation
Hide the Bar at the Bottom
Submitted by Sam Brannen

1. Press Ctrl + Alt + S to make the bar at the bottom of Navigator's window disappear.

2. Press the Ctrl + Alt + S combination again to restore it.

Netscape Navigator 2.0
Netscape Communications Corporation
Status Report of Active URLs
Submitted by Marko Faas

1. Simply press Ctrl + Alt + T in combination.

Application Easter Eggs

Netscape Navigator 3.0
Netscape Communications Corporation
Intra-Office Memo
Submitted by Allan Wax

1. Type "about:about" in the Location field.

2. Press Enter.

3. Read a message from one Netscape worker to another.

Norton Antivirus for Windows 95
Symantec Corporation
The Virus Hunters
Submitted by Luis Alonso Ramos

1. In Norton Antivirus, select **About** from the **Help** menu.

2. Press N + A + V simultaneously. A dialog box with a picture of the development team will appear.

3. Press Esc to close this box.

Norton Commander 95
Symantec Corporation
Photo Egg
Submitted by Zdravko Ruzicic

1. Choose **Help**.

2. Choose **About**.

3. Press ⌈Ctrl⌋ while double-clicking the icon.

4. A large photo of the programming team appears.

Norton Desktop for Windows
Symantec Corporation
More than a Thousand Words
Submitted by Douglas Ghormley

1. Select **About** from the **Help** menu.

2. Click three times while holding down ⌊N⌋ + ⌊D⌋ + ⌊W⌋ .

3. You should see a picture of the developers with quotations.

189

Norton Utilities 8.0
Symantec Corporation
Photo Screen
Submitted by Cousin Bug

1. Open any Windows Norton Utilities application.

2. Select **Help \ About**.

3. Press Ⓝ + Ⓤ + ⑧.

4. Look at the developers. Move the mouse around!

Norton Utilities 9 for Windows 95
Symantec Corporation
Team Photo
Submitted by Geoffrey W. Schreiber

1. Open any application for Norton Utilities 9.

2. Open the About box.

3. Press Ⓝ + Ⓤ + ⑨.

Oracle Book v.2.0 and 2.1
Oracle Corporation
Music and Welcome
Submitted by Scott Stephens

1. Select **About Oracle Book** from the menu.

2. Click on the Oracle Book icon.

3. First it will display the names of the original developers, then it will play some Dylan, say "Welcome to Oracle Book" and play some Simon and Garfunkle.

4. This will not work in character mode; there are no icons or sound in character mode.

PageMaker 5.0
Aldus
Dedication
Submitted by Andy Banks

1. Hold down the [Shift] button.

2. Go to **Help**.

3. Select **About PageMaker**.

4. That's it. You should see a dedication to one of the head programmers of PageMaker 4.0.

PageMaker 6.0

Adobe Systems, Incorporated
See the Software Team
Submitted by William Johnson

1. Open PageMaker 6.0

2. Hold down `Ctrl` + `Shift`.

3. Go to the **Help** menu and select **About PageMaker**.

4. When the screen comes up wait two-three seconds and Voila!

Photoshop 3.0

Adobe Systems Incorporated
April Fool
Submitted by Ken Wright

1. Change your computer's timer to April first, of any year.

2. Start Photoshop as usual to see a new startup screen.

Photoshop 4.0
Adobe Systems Incorporated
Official Mascot
Submitted by GJP

1. Click on **Help/About Photoshop…**, holding [Alt] while releasing the mouse button.

2. Or, hold [Alt] while you click the "eyecon" atop the floating toolbar.

3. The mascot's creator is listed in the credits.

Photoshop
Adobe Systems Incorporated
Merlin
Submitted by Marc McNaughton

1. Open Photoshop normally.

2. Open any pallet that has "pallet options" (layers, paths, etc.).

3. Hold down [Alt], click on the pallet menu and select "Pallet Options."

4. Merlin will appear, next to a flower.

5. Click the "Begone" button to make him disappear.

Photoshop v.3.0.5
Adobe Systems Incorporated
Silly Messages
Submitted by Tan Chun Ghee and Chia Jiun Wei

1. Go to **Help/About Adobe Photoshop...**.

2. Wait while the credits start rolling. You may press Alt to speed them by.

3. At the end are some really dumb comments.

4. But that's not all! Wait for the credits to end and restart.

5. Now hold down Ctrl + Shift and click on the Adobe logo.

6. Ta-da!

Powerpoint 4.0
(Microsoft Corporation)
Developer Credits
Submitted by Susie Ehrenfeld

1. Click on **About MS Powerpoint**.

2. Click anywhere on the box that appears.

3. The box will then change to list the developers.

Powerpoint 97
(Microsoft Corporation)
The Team
Submitted by Junben Bajuyo

1. Launch Powerpoint 97.

2. Select **Help/About**.

3. Click on the Powerpoint icon.

Prodigy
Prodigy Services Corporation
Picture of the Developers
Submitted by Mr. Galakeewich

1. Start the service.

2. Once you're at highlights, press [Shift], [Shift], [Alt], [Alt], [Ctrl] and [Ctrl] + [9] in sequence using the left side of the keyboard.

Qbasic
(Microsoft Corporation)
Team Colours
Submitted by Benjamin Tay

1. Start Qbasic by entering "QBASIC" at the command prompt.

2. Immediately hold down both `Shift`, both `Alt` and both `Ctrl` keys simultaneously.

3. Wait just a few seconds. The team credits should come up in a cool and colourful manner.

QuickTime v.2.1.1.57—16 bit
Apple Computer, Incorporated
Hidden Picture
Submitted by Jeff Withers

1. Start the QuickTime Control Panel.

2. Double-click the QuickTime icon.

3. Under the Setup tab, click the QuickTime logo.

4. Click the right mouse button anywhere inside the about box.

Application Easter Eggs

Quicken
Intuit
Animation and Credits
Submitted by Alan Hamilton

1. To see the versions of the Quicken components, hold [Shift] as you select **Help \ About**.

2. Various animations are hidden in the **Help \ About** box. Select **Help \ About** (without [Shift]) and press one of the following keys.

3. **R**: Rattlesnake animation

4. **S**: Credits

5. **V**: Extended version information

6. **P**: Intuit logo animation (may not work in v. 5)

Turbo Pascal for Windows
Borland International, Incorporated
Those Responsible
Submitted by Andrew Widdowson

1. In Turbo Pascal for Windows, go into the **Help** menu.

2. Select **About**.

3. Press [Alt] + [T].

4. You should see a scrolling list of those responsible for bringing Turbo Pascal to you.

Visual C++ 2.0+
(Microsoft Corporation)
3D Flying
Submitted by John Ridley

1. Go to the **Help** menu and select **About**.

2. Hold [Ctrl] and double-click on the graphic.

3. Release [Ctrl] at the same time the second click is released.

4. Use the keypad, [A] and [Z] to fly around pictures of the developers.

Visual C++ 2.2, 4.0
(Microsoft Corporation)
Spin or Fly
Submitted by John Ridley

1. Put the VC++ CD-ROM into your CD-ROM drive.

2. Start VC++.

3. Select **About** from the **Help** menu.

4. Hold down the [Ctrl] button.

5. Double-left click, releasing the [Ctrl] button exactly when you release the left mouse button.

6. VC++ 2.2 spins a plus sign for you, with programmer credits.

7. VC++ 4.0 lets you fly around a landscape made up of programmer's photos.

Visual C++ 2.2
(Microsoft Corporation)
Passcount Breakpoints
Submitted by Ben Levy

1. Add "/bppassc:yes" to the command line for MSVC (using the PIF editor).

2. Start MSVC, select **break points**, and now you can set a passcount for break points.

Visual Basic 4.0
(Microsoft Corporation)
Thunder
Submitted by Michael

1. Add a test box to a form.

2. Change its text property to "Thunder."

3. Lock the control on the form.

4. Move the mouse over the tools in the toolbox.

5. Instead of the usual tool tips, you should see the names of the developers and testers.

Word
(Microsoft Corporation)
Word Squashes Wordperfect
Submitted by Douglas Ghormley

1. Open a new document.

2. From the **Tools** menu, select **Macro...**, then click **Record**.

3. Create a macro named "Spiff" and click **OK**.

4. Stop the recorder, and highlight **Spiff**.

5. Select **Edit** and delete the "Sub Main" and "End" sublines.

6. Under the **File** menu, select **Close** and click **Yes**.

7. Go to the **Help** menu, select **About** and click on the Word logo.

Word for Windows 6.0
(Microsoft Corporation)
Personal Thanks
Submitted by Susie Ehrenfeld

1. In a new document, type "t3!"

2. Bold the whole word.

3. Choose **Autoformat** from the **Format** menu.

4. Click **OK**, then **Accept**.

Continued on next page

5. Select **About Microsoft Word...** from the **Help** menu.

6. Click the Word logo in the upper-left corner and watch the credits.

7. If you're patient enough to wait until the end (about a minute and a half), you'll receive mention in the credits (if this copy of Word is registered in your name).

Word 7.0

(Microsoft Corporation)

Blue

Submitted by Raul Heiduk

---

1. Open a new document.

2. Type "Blue."

3. Select this word.

4. Choose "Font..." from the **Format** menu.

5. Select "Bold" as the style and "Blue" as the color.

6. Type one space after the word "Blue."

7. Open the About box from the **Help** menu.

8. Watch for a special name at the end of the list.

Word 97
(Microsoft Corporation)
Pinball Productivity Application
Submitted by Kevin Arima

1. Open a new document.

2. Type "Blue."

3. Select this word.

4. Choose "Font..." from the **Format** menu.

5. Select "Bold" as the style and "Blue" as the color.

6. Type one space after the word "Blue."

7. Open the About box from the **Help** menu.

8. Hold [Ctrl] + [Shift] and left-click the Word icon.

9. Use [Z] and [M] for flippers. [Esc] will exit the "productivity application."

Application Easter Eggs

Word 7.0
(Microsoft Corporation)
Clover Cursor
Submitted by Aries M Castillo

1. Open Word.

2. Press Ctrl + Alt + +.

3. The mouse pointer should change to a clover leaf.

4. If this doesn't work, select **Help/About...** and repeat step two.

Word Pro
(Lotus Development Corporation)
Developers' Doom
Submitted by Me

1. Bring up the About box (Help/About Word Pro).

2. Spell the word "possum" by clicking the appropriate letters in the yellow "Lotus Word Pro" at the top of the box.

3. In other words, click on the "P," then an "o," then "s" twice and then "u."

4. After you click on the "u," an opossum will walk out. Click on its butt right under his tail (this can be tricky; if you miss, start over from the beginning).

5. The opossum will lay an egg with the letter "m" on it. Click this "m."

Continued on next page

6. A Doom-like 3D world will appear. You can move around with the arrow keys, Shift and Alt, just like Doom.

7. Press Esc or click OK to exit the egg.

Word Viewer 7.1
(Microsoft Corporation)
Developer Credits
Submitted by Alan Ford

---

1. Go to **Help/About...**.

2. Hold down Ctrl + Shift and click on the logo.

Games
Easter Eggs

Buried in Time
(Sanctuary Woods)
Moonwalking Agent
Submitted by Cindy

1. Go to Leonardo da Vinci's time period.

2. Unlock the door to the balcony with the key (found in the keyhole).

3. Hold Ctrl as you go through the door.

4. The enemy agent will dance and moonwalk until you release the Ctrl key.

Buried in Time
(Sanctuary Woods)
Da Vinci's Bad Side
Submitted by Brian Cubbage

1. Go to Leonardo da Vinci's studio.

2. Make your way to the workshop. Walk up to the cabinet on the very left of the row of cabinets.

3. Go close to the sign and use the translator biochip to read Leonardo's note.

DOS Civilization

(MicroProse)

Access the Entire Map

Submitted by Balto

1. Hold [Shift] and type "1234567890."

2. You can now look into enemy cities.

3. You can unfortify their units.

4. You can sell their improvements.

5. You can rearrange their resources.

6. You can view the power chart and the replay.

Civ Net

(MicroProse)

A Cheat Menu

Submitted by David Stevenson

1. Wait until the end-turn light is flashing.

2. Press [Ctrl] and release it.

3. Type "aodbamf."

4. A menu of available cheats will appear.

Command and Conquer: Covert Operations
(Westwood Studios)
Dinosaurs
Submitted by Patrick

1. At the DOS prompt in the C&C directory, type "C&C funpark."

2. Choose to start a new game and you'll be playing against dinosaurs.

DarkForces
(Lucas Arts)
Find an Ewok
Submitted by Tim Gray

1. Once you're in level ten, turn on the god mode cheat (type "laimlame").

2. Jump down into the pit next to where you start.

3. Now keep trying to open a secret door. Try every wall. You should enter a room with a chain in the middle of it.

4. Try opening another secret door in the walls. There you should find an ewok who does weird things.

Doom II
(Id Software)

Select your Music

Submitted by Justin Rodante

1. Type "idmus#" where "#" equals any number between zero and 36 to play the music written for that level.

Thinkin' Things
(Edmark)

Author! Author!

Submitted by Nick Newhard

1. In the setup program select a sound card without recording capability.

2. Run Thinkin' Things and select the Blox module.

3. Press [Ctrl] + [Alt] + [Shift] and click on the blank button normally reserved for recording.

4. The author's name will appear in flashing colors.

Earthworm Jim
(Activision)

The Early Worm Gets the Credit

Submitted by Daniel Silo

1. From anywhere in the game, type "iddqd" or "idkfa."

2. The game will pause and display the credit screens.

Exile II: Crystal Souls
(Jeff Vogel)
Secret Location
Submitted by Tuan Bui

1. Go to the Tower of the Magi, in the southeast.

2. Go to the teleporter room (you'll need magi clearance).

3. When it asks for coordinates, type "Eas Ter Egg."

Flight Simulator 6
(Microsoft Corporation)
Headquarters
Submitted by Carlos De Sedas

1. Start the FS6 program.

2. On the menu click "World/Set Exact Location."

3. Set latitude/longitude to N047° 39' 23" W122° 08' 40.5", altitude to 0ft, heading 340 degrees.

4. You are now in front of one of the buildings at the MS campus in Redmond, WA.

5. Hit Y to start slew mode and press 8 on the keypad about three times and roll into the lobby.

6. When you're inside and see the photo mural on the wall, press 5 on the keypad.

7. The picture will toggle photos of some of the FS6 team.

Flight Unlimited
(Looking Glass Technologies, Incorporated)
MechGodzilla Instructor
Submitted by Jeff Justiz

1. Start flying a lesson.

2. Press Ⓜ + Ⓖ + Ⓔₛc.

3. Your instructor will become MechGodzilla (talk about having someone **bark** orders at you!).

Leisure Suit Larry 7: Love for Sail!
(Sierra On-Line, Incorporated)
Dream Sequence
Submitted by Cedric Henry

1. Go to Captain Queeg's ballroom.

2. Type "dream" in the "other" section when you click on yourself.

Mechwarrior 2
(Activision)
Programmers
Anonymous submission

1. In the ice caves, click on the left hanging light.

2. In the drop ship, click on the monitor to the right of and below the mission computer.

3. Either of these will display the programmers of Mechwarrior 2.

Mechwarrior 2
(Activision)
Art Designers and More
Submitted by Michael A. Paine

1. Go to Clan Jade Falcon.

2. Go to the archive computer.

3. Click on all the numbers on the left.

4. When you click on certain numbers, menus pop up.

5. This will work for Clan Wolf, also.

Mechwarrior 2
(Activision)
Another Place to Meet the Programmers
Submitted by Edward Wei

1. Go to the mercenary commander option at the very beginning or the game.

2. Log yourself into the terminal.

3. Go to the office.

4. Go to the MechBay.

5. At the MechBay click on the second or third light on the ceiling down the right-hand hallway.

Monty Python and the Search for the Holy Grail
(7th Level, Incorporated)
Remove the Leaf
Submitted by Lawrence Stowbunenko

1. Go to the witch scene.

2. Type "noleaf."

3. Click on the witch until she flashes.

4. The leaf is gone!

Phantasmagoria
(Sierra On-Line)
In the Baby's Room...
Submitted by Federico Cavazos

1. This works in all chapters except chapter one. Go to the Baby's room on the third floor.

2. Rapidly click on the picture of the baby hanging on the wall.

3. If you do this correctly the baby's eyes will start to glow and you will hear a psycho laugh.

Phantasmagoria
(Sierra On-Line)
Staff
Submitted by David Baker

1. In Curtis' home, click on the picture next to the book case to see the programming staff.

Phantasmagoria
(Sierra On-Line)
Washroom Sounds
Submitted by W. Manning

1. You must do this the first time Adrienne uses the washroom.

2. Click on the bathroom chair seven times before clicking on the toilet.

3. There are several variants of this. To try them all, save the game prior to step one and then retry.

Quake
(Id Software)

Nightmare Super Secret

Submitted by Robert Swan

1. Enter episode four from the introduction.

2. Jump into the pool with the false bottom.

3. Before you fall through, turn 180 degrees and head for the left corner. Then drop through.

4. You should land on the wooden beam. Follow this to the doorway.

5. Go through the hallway and shoot at the glowing skulls picture. You will get a secret message about the "Well of Wishes."

6. Jump to episode two, "Crypt of Decay."

7. Find the Well of Wishes for a surprise.

Quake
(Id Software)
Secret level: Ziggurat Vertigo
Submitted by MadDog

1. In episode one, mission four (the Grisly Grotto), dispose of the ogres in the room with blue slime then ride the platform up to the next floor.

2. Step (carefully) onto each of the floorplates in this room to open two secret doors.

3. Go through each of these doors and press the button on the ledge where you land. You will see a message about a secret cave opening.

4. Go back to the deep pool in the room where you got (or will get) the silver key. On your right (if you are facing the door at the end of the pier) is a submerged well-lit cave entrance. Swim into it and up to find goodies and a slipgate.

5. This slipgate will take you to Ziggurat Vertigo, which can be a "high flying" adventure.

Quake
(Id Software)

Secret level: Underearth

Submitted by MadDog

1. At the last intersection of episode two, mission three (the Crypt of Decay), you may go right to the level exit or left to a room with boxes. Go to the room with boxes and shoot the switch in the ceiling.

2. This will open a secret door above the boxes. Go through this door for a treat and press the button.

3. This button opens an underwater barrier. If you have already been there, go again and skip to the last step. If you haven't been there, go back to the area where you picked up the gold key (just beyond the spike trap).

4. Shoot the back wall of the alcove on your right to open a secret door.

5. Jump into the water and pick up the goodies.

6. You can see that the barrier has been removed and you can now swim through the portal. Do so and ascend the ramp to the teleporter to the Underearth.

Quake
(Id Software)
Secret level: The Haunted Halls
Submitted by MadDog

1. Near the end of episode three, mission four (Satan's Dark Delight) you descend a stairway with a lightning gun at the bottom.

2. Look under the stairs. You will see a pair of ledges overlooking a hole.

3. Leap into this hole and you will land in the Haunted Halls.

Quake
(Id Software)
Secret level: The Nameless City
Submitted by MadDog

1. In episode four, mission five (The Elder World), you need the silver key to activate a bridge leading to the exit. Get this key but don't activate the bridge.

2. Instead, hop across the lava via the bridge's support poles.

3. Once across, use the silver key to pass through the giant door on the left, which leads to the Nameless City.

Games Easter Eggs

Rebel Assault II
(Lucas Arts)
Cheat Access and Animation
Submitted by Rob (Not "Bob")

1. On starting Rebel Assault, when the Lucas Arts logo is spinning, point the joystick rapidly to each corner of the screen, clicking the joystick fire button once in each corner.

2. If done right, you'll hear a ringing bell and a goofy "Luuucasss Artsss" chant. You'll also have access to game cheats for the rest of the session.

3. After winning the game (or warping to level 16), after watching the credits, look for the silly animation.

4. May the force be with you!

Rebel Assault II
(Lucas Arts)
Martinez Outake
Submitted by Evil the Cat

1. At the pilot screen, make a new pilot and name him Gary Martinez.

2. Start the game as regular.

Rebel Assault II
(Lucas Arts)
More Outakes
Submitted by Joaquim Martinez (with thanks to Evil the Cat)

1. Start a new game.

2. Enter the name of someone from the credits as the pilot's name. Try Vince Lee, Richard Green, Hal Barwood, Brian Kemp, Doug Shannon, Jamison Jones, Julie Eccles, Carl Magruder, Tamlynn Barra, Aaron Muszalski, John Knoles, Clint Young, Larry the O, Sth Piezas, Peter McConnell, Chris Weakley and Steve Dauterman.

Rebel Assault II
(Lucas Arts)
Chorus Line Stormtroopers
Submitted by Derek Lieu

1. Go to level 12, "the sewers."

2. Kill all the stormtroopers.

3. After the last trooper in section four is dead, hold down Ⓐ + Ⓒ + Ⓣ until the elevator closes.

Rise of the Triad
(Apogee Software, Inc.)
Holiday Mode
Submitted by Kevin Chulski

1. Boot up Rise of the Triad on Christmas day (or change your computer's date so it believes it's Christmas day).

2. Start a level and it should play Christmas music.

3. One of the heroes will also have a red cap on his head.

4. Similar things happen on other major holidays—try them all!

SimAnt
(Maxis)
Morph to Spider
Submitted by Ming-Fu Hsu

1. Click on yellow ant.

2. Press X.

3. Click on the head of the spider.

SimCity
(Maxis)

Not Guilty

Submitted by David

1. Type "o.j."

2. Go to city book.

3. Type "free."

4. This will allow your city to fabulously operate with no traffic, crime, pollution or unemployment.

SimCity 2000
(Maxis)

Debug Menu

Submitted by Bao Nguyen

1. Load SimCity 2000. You don't have to have a new city.

2. Click on the bar of the toolbar. You can do this only in city building mode, not in landscape shaping.

3. Type "oivaizmir."

4. You should notice an extra menu called "Debug" that contains another menu called "Debug" that contains many different items.

SimCity 2000
(Maxis)
One Word Wonders
Submitted by Kevin

1. Type "heck," "damn" or "darn" in the program to see a funny message.

2. Type "vers" to see the version number of the software.

3. Type "porn" to hear the programmer moan, "Can't get enough."

4. Type "memy" to check the computer's memory.

SimCity 2000
(Maxis)
Helicopter Crash
Submitted by Martin Deutsch

1. Run Sim City with a helicopter hovering around (i.e., build an airport).

2. Select the centering tool.

3. Click on the center of the helicopter.

4. If you aimed successfully, the pilot will say "I'm hit!" and "Mayday!" before crashing his whirlybird.

SimCity 2000
(Maxis)

Churches, Churches

Submitted by Tim Kerby

1. Save your game (unless it's a friend's game).

2. Type "heck," "damn" or "darn."

3. Wait for it...

4. Every bit of dense residential area that fits a church will get one. And you can't reverse the process.

SimTower
(Maxis)

Big Lobby

Submitted by Bao Nguyen

1. Start a new game of SimTower.

2. Select Lobby.

3. Hold Ctrl while building a lobby. This will build a two-story lobby.

4. Hold Ctrl + Shift while building a lobby to make it three stories tall.

5. The escalators and stairs will look big and cool!

SimCity Urban Renewal Kit
(Maxis)
Dancing Arcology
Anonymous Submission

1. Enter SCURK.

2. Type "VAUDEVILLE."

3. Watch the dancing arco.

SimCopter
(Maxis)
Apache
Submitted by Jason Mann

1. Press Ctrl + Alt + X.

2. Type "I'm the CEO of McDonnel Douglas."

3. Go to hanger.

4. Go to the place you buy helicopters.

5. Press 3.

6. Go outside.

7. Find the Apache and climb in.

8. If you can't find it, try it in a city without military.

9. Go to a nuclear power plant, press T and fire twice to create a nuclear meltdown.

Torin's Passage
(Sierra On-Line, Incorporated)
Al Lowe's Message
Submitted by Cedric Henry

1. Get all the way to Lysentia's lair.

2. Us the bagpipes on her.

3. Listen!

US Navy Fighters 1.2 or US Navy Fighters Gold
(Electric Arts)
Fly an Atomic Moth
Submitted by Wally Anglesea

1. Hold `Alt` + `Ctrl` + Right-`Shift` throughout this process.

2. Select **Fly Quick Mission**.

3. Select all of the options you want to have on the mission.

4. Select **Atomic Moth** as your aircraft.

5. Make sure you are still holding the `Alt` + `Ctrl` + Right-`Shift` combination and click `OK`.

6. You can release the key combination now and enjoy the mission. FYI: It takes lots of Atomic Mothballs to destroy a TU Bear.

Warcraft II: Beyond the Dark Portal
(Blizzard Entertainment)
Hidden Song
Submitted by Alex Planes

1. Press [Enter].

2. Type "disco."

3. Press [Enter] again.

Warcraft II: Beyond the Dark Portal
(Blizzard Entertainment)
Make the units talk, sing and scold
Submitted by James Overbeck

1. Left-click any unit.

2. Repeatedly left-click it while holding the pointer on it.

3. Continue left-clicking. Each unit so clicked will cycle through all the phrases it can possibly say until it has said them all.

Warcraft II: Beyond the Dark Portal
(Blizzard Entertainment)
Exploding Critters
Submitted by Ehh

1. Click on a critter.

2. Now click it again.

3. Now click it a lot!

4. BOOM!!!

Wing Commander III
(Origin)
Movies and Quotes
Submitted by Paul O'Brien

1. Go to the options screen before the load screen with the big star surrounded by other little stars (load this from CDs 2-4, not CD 1).

2. Double-click on the little stars in this order: upper right, lower left, upper left, lower right. This takes you to a credits sequence with funny quotes from the designers.

3. During the opening scene, hold down [Shift] + [Del] + [F10] and type "LordBritish" to go to an options screen where you can view any movie sequence in the game.

Wing Commander IV
(Origin)
Cool Stuff
Submitted by Zack Newton

1. Start a new game.

2. Go through the first mission.

3. Access the terminal before the second mission.

4. When the grey letters are on the screen, before it asks for your callsign, enter:

5. "Animal" to get a game within your game.

6. "Chicken" to see a new version of the credits with Moe and Bart.

Wolfenstein 3D
(Id Software)
?
Submitted by Jonathan H.

1. Open Wolfenstein 3D.

2. When you get to the Id screen, press Ⓑ.

Zork Nemesis
(Activision)
Photograph
Submitted by Michael

1. Type "chloe" anywhere in the game.

2. This will transport you to the library. Open a book and open to the first page.

3. Look at the beautiful programmer(?).

Zork Nemesis
(Activision)
What's Happening?
Submitted by Michael

1. Type "hello sailor."

2. In earlier Zork games this was a foul curse and usually resulted in some sort of humorous or not-so-humorous penalty.

3. In Nemesis a woman's voice says, "Nothing happens here."

Alphabetical Listing

The following is an alphabetical listing of the Easter eggs that you'll find described in pages 127-232. For an index of the entire book, see pages 239-242.

236

Index

Index

240

Index

V

W

PC catalog

Order Toll Free 1-800-451-4319
Books and Software

Includes CD-ROM with Sample Programs

Abacus

Multimedia Presentation

PC Photography Book

The PC Photography Book is for all camera buffs, home users, hobbyists, desktop publishers, graphic artists, marketing communication professionals and multimedia enthusiasts.

Many companies, including Kodak, Seattle FilmWorks, Storm Software, Delrina, Hewlett-Packard and others, are pioneering a new consumer level technology which lets you move common photos or snap shots onto your PC. Digital imaging software and graphic gear is easier to use, more affordable and the quality of output excellent.

PC Photography starts with the basics of image processing and taking quality photos. A special treatment is given to Kodak's photo CD format that allows anyone to put photos on CD-ROM. The technology and process are both explained in depth. It then moves on to examine how today's hardware and software work—both the digital camera and the photo reader.

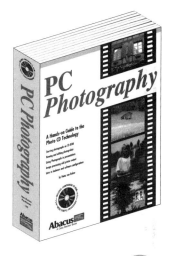

Includes CD-ROM with Sample Programs

Learn how to work with: Micrografx PhotoMagic, Microsoft Publisher, CorelDraw, Aldus Freehand and Photostyler, and Adobe PhotoShop.

The companion CD-ROM includes samplers of:

- Toshiba's Photo/Graphic Viewer
- MicroTek's Photo Star graphic utility
- PCD photo examples used in the book
- Collection of popular shareware graphics utilities including:
  - JASC'S PaintShop Pro
  - Graphics WorkShop
- Several industry standard Phillips CD-I software drivers

Author: Heinz von Buelow and Dirk Paulissen
Order Item: #B293
ISBN: 1-55755-293-2

SRP: $34.95 US/$46.95 CAN includes CD-ROM

To order direct call Toll Free 1-800-451-4319

In US and Canada add $5.00 shipping and handling. Foreign orders add $13.00 per item.
Michigan residents add 6% sales tax.

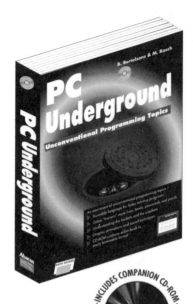

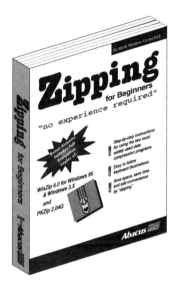

Software

ZIP KIT

Learn to Use the World's Most Popular Data Compression Programs!

Start Using WinZip and nine other fully functional evaluation versions of the most popular data compression shareware in the universe today.

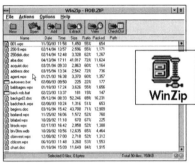

PKZip

ARJ

LH-ICE

WinZip

PKLite

LHArc

LZH

This Windows-based utility makes unlocking the treasures of the information superhighway a breeze. Zip and unzip. Drag-and-drop. Virus scanning support.

Graphic & Video Utilities

Special graphic and video programs in the **ZIP KIT** will help you work with dozens of different formats.

Learn to convert and compress numerous graphic formats with unique image processing software: ART, BMP, DIB, GIF, IFF, ICO, LBM, MSP, PCX, RLE, TIF, WPG, CUT, EXE, HRZ, IMG, JPG, MAC, PIC, RAS, TGA, and TXT.

Discover the world of compressed video files: FLI, AVI, MPG, FLC, and MCI.

ZIP KIT
Item #S287   **SRP: $34.95 US/ $46.95 CAN**
ISBN 1-55755-290-8
UPC 0 90869 55290 1

To order direct call Toll Free 1-800-451-4319

In US and Canada add $5.00 shipping and handling. Foreign orders add $13.00 per item. Michigan residents add 6% sales tax.

Software

Pilot's Shop
for Microsoft Flight Simulator
Aircraft, Scenery & Utilities

Pilot's Shop is a new CD-ROM collection of the world's best add-ons for Microsoft Flight Simulator. This new CD-ROM instantly makes flying even more authentic and exciting as you travel virtually anywhere.

New Planes—fly new powerful and classic planes form the past.

Fly new and modified planes to new locations, plan detailed flights, make precision landings and build your own sceneries using sophisticated tools.

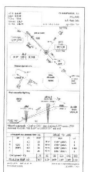

Flight Planners and Approach Plates—plot and print your own graphical maps and step-by-step plans with way-points help you plan short flights or transoceanic trips and realistic precision instrument landings.

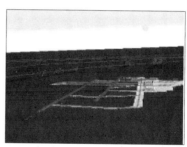

New Impressive Scenery— fly to new destinations—exciting Las Vegas, adventurous Grand Tetons, exotic Hong Kong, lovely France, Canada, Scotland, Switzerland, Vietnam and more!

Pilot's Shop
Item #S308
ISBN 1-55755-308-4
UPC 0 90869 55308 3

SRP: 29.95 USA/$39.95 CAN

To order direct call Toll Free 1-800-451-4319

In US and Canada add $5.00 shipping and handling. Foreign orders add $13.00 per item.
Michigan residents add 6% sales tax.

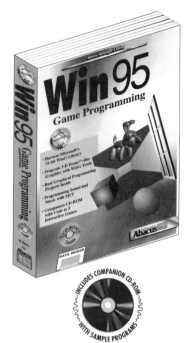

About This Book

Today, Easter eggs have almost attained "feature" status among software developers. Products seem incomplete if they don't contain an egg or two. In this age of megacorporations and huge design teams for single programs, Easter eggs have become a way for programmers to put some personality back into the software.

I have tried to go beyond a simple listing of Easter eggs with this book. This is a history of the Easter egg world and how they have evolved in complexity and humor over the years. Here are tips on how to find Easter eggs yourself, with methods catagorized by difficulty so you can find them whether you're a computer virgin or regularly do binary math in your head.

> One of the great things about Easter eggs is that you don't always have to find them yourself!

You will also be taken into the depths of the programming community to see how Easter eggs are conceived. Included are some rare glimpses of eggs that were intercepted by management and never saw the light of day

One of the great things about Easter eggs is that you don't always have to find them yourself! Thousands of other Easter egg hunters help you track them down every day. Thanks to the great communication medium of the Internet, we Easter egg lovers can easily share our knowledge. If you don't feel like searching for eggs yourself, don't worry! Plenty of us out here are far more obsessed than you may be, and you can benefit from our efforts.

The second part of this book is an indexed list of all the PC Easter eggs I know about. From Adobe to Zork, if there is an egg I know about, it's in here. Check this list before you start hunting on your own; it will save you a lot of time and effort.

So sit back, and enjoy the lighter side of software for a while. You'll discover that programmers like a good laugh as much as the rest of us.